George R Parburt

Anselmo

A Poem

George R Parburt

Anselmo
A Poem

ISBN/EAN: 9783744704458

Printed in Europe, USA, Canada, Australia, Japan

Cover: Foto ©Thomas Meinert / pixelio.de

More available books at **www.hansebooks.com**

ANSELMO:

A POEM.

BY GEORGE R. PARBURT.

SAN FRANCISCO
H. H. BANCROFT & COMPANY.
1865.

Entered according to Act of Congress, in the year 1865, by GEORGE R. PARBURT, in the Clerk's office of the District Court of the Northern District of California.

VANDALL, CARR & CO., PRINTERS.

ERRATA.

Page 27, verse 67—for "Oh," read "On."
" 28, " 70—for "riseth on," read "rise upon."
" 29, " 73—for "behold, read "beheld."
" 42, " 25—for "Day-good," read "Day-God."
" 50, " 48—for "angel's," read "angelic."
" 61, " 83—for "goodly," read "godly."
" 62, " 86—for "love-stolen," read "love's stolen."
" 71, " 9—for "floated," read "floateth."
" 89, " 55—for "revivng," read "reviving."
" 93, " 68—for "shown," read "shone."
" 98, " 1—for "humid," read "lurid."
" 114, " 48—for "horsemen," read "horseman."
" 133, " 27—for "blast," read "blest."

To Leila.

Some years ago,—how many—matters not
    To others; by ourselves remembered well;
While lingering near a favorite trysting spot,
    There was a promise made;—why? Who shall tell?
Enough for us, it hath not been forgot;
    On its performance let your favor dwell:
The promise was,—ANSELMO,—then a dream,
Should don the habit of a living theme.

At the first glance you may not recognize
    The fondling of our days of young romance;
For he hath grown in gracefulness and size,
    Like children who are early taught to dance;
But whoso shall his features scrutinize,
    And make allowances for life's advance,
Will doubtless be quite fully satisfied
The child is in the man identified.

Doth it not argue weakness to forestall
    A smile of irony and tone sarcastic?
"And call you this ANSELMO? Is this all
    Of that erratic genius once so plastic?"
Patience, my LEILA—take the gift, though small:
    It is not guileful, nor is it bombastic.—
ANSELMO hath no mysteries to unravel:
So, having made his debut—let him travel.

ANSELMO.

CANTO FIRST.

I.

THE Age of Gold warms not with themes of Love;
   It throbs not with the impulse of Desire;
The Vulture is its emblem, not the Dove;
   To prey, and not to praise, doth it aspire:
Banks are its temples—not the living grove;
   Friendship and Faith are victims of its fire:
It stamps each virtue of the human breast
With the adulterous face of interest.

II.

The clink of Mammon is the tone extatic
   Of this Cash Age, yclept Utilitarian;
In which all elements, grave and erratic,
   Forsake Elysia to become Agrarian:
Air, water, fire, in labors are pragmatic;
   The glorious Sun a wandering Daguerrean;
The lightning flits away from heaven, with joy,
To outstrip Time as Traffic's errand-boy.

III.

Presumptuous Age! Well may the timid Moon
   Wrap her soft features up in cloudy sadness,
Lest in thy vanity to play the loon,
   Thou shouldst, with gravely mercenary madness,
Profane her charms, by offering them a boon
   To dusky Labor in his steaming gladness;
Making her beams a power to grind a grist on,
To whirl a spindle, or to drive a piston.

IV.

There was a time when Luna did inspire
   In blooming vales, on mountain top and ocean,
Brave youth and Beauty with profound desire,
   To analyze that hallowing devotion,
Shekina of love's lip-enkindled fire,
   Which throbs the heart with rapturous emotion:
Wild, as Euroclydon at midnight hour—
Gentle, as Zephyrus in Flora's bower.

V.

When pensive lovers, lest their love should moulder,
   Sought the new moon for timely consolation,
And gazing at her, over the right shoulder,
   Renewed their vows of endless adoration;
Till moon-like, nightly waxing warm and bolder—
   Fraught with the pleasures of anticipation—
They sought, they found, Love's charming ideality
Excelleth far the raptures of reality.

VI.

Maugre the Age! Love is my theme of Song;
    A youth the hero of my untaught lay;
Who whilom dwelt, where grandly flows along
    The proud Potomac through Columbia;
He shunned alike the vain and busy throng
    Of crafty commerce and gay revelry;
To woo in sylvan solitudes a muse,
Whose charms imbued his mind with pensive hues.

VII.

Oft-times he wander'd through the classic grounds,
    His cherished Alma Mater yet adorning;
And often, where the river wildly bounds
    Over rock and chasm, like a sprite forewarning,
Rapt as a babe whom slumberous dreams surround
    With blissful visions, he would muse till morning,
Drinking deep draughts from that eternal ocean,
Where stars renew their glory and devotion.

VIII.

And so ANSELMO thought for aye to find
    The scene unchanging, and unchanged his dream
Of mental joys, which charm the youthful mind,
    And with the purer lights of science beam;
He knew not that an ever-varying wind
    And chainless tide control Time's rapid stream,
Dashing, in its alternate ebb and flow,
Life's cup of joy with bitter draughts of woe.

IX.

There was a flower, a beautiful wild flower,
    Whose bloom and fragrance warm'd his soul with love;
And he had lingered by it many an hour—
    Had gazed upon it, as the Saints above
Gaze on the Throne of Light: he had no power,
    No wish to pluck it from its native grove.
His gaze was pure and lofty admiration;
His love the holy flame of adoration.

X.

He saw its tender sepals softly springing,
    In velvet leaflets from its balmy bud;
He watched the vernal sunbeams daily bringing
    Light as the rainbow bending o'er the flood,
Sweet as the harmonies of Angels singing,
    Rich as the blushes of the fair and good—
The tints of heaven, and its immortal dews,
To enrich its petals with diviner hues.

XI.

He did not dream his heart was touched with love;
    He had not even thought what love might be;
Books were his pride; and his delight, to prove
    This earth, with all its rivers and its sea,
Its continents, where living myriads rove,
    A point, an atom in immensity:
The starry skies only a brilliant verse,
In the grand epic of the universe.

XII.

By toilsome process doth the mind attain
  The ruder outlines of unpolished lore;
While with severer discipline, the brain
  Delves from the mines of knowledge richer ore,
And smelts the crude mass o'er and o'er again,
  Ere it doth form and fashion thoughts mature,
And in its own creations can combine
The strength and beauty of an art divine.

XIII.

Not so the heart—the strange, impulsive heart;
  It hath no seasons for maturity;
No discipline doth by degrees impart
  To it the lore of self-security;
When nature gives the signal for the start,
  With all the zeal of conscious purity,
It boundeth, full-formed, from its native skies,
To win the goal and grasp the hallowed prize:

XIV.

A bud, at once expanding to full flower;
  A spring, diffusing quickly to an ocean;
A hidden spark, charged with volcanic power;
  A thought, all tremulous with profound emotion;
An embryo, maturing in an hour;
  Desire, burning with sublime devotion:
Alike in youth and age, with smile and tear,
It throbs, the wild extremes of hope and fear.

XV.

Dear to ANSELMO was the fairy child;
   The sole companion of his happy hours;
Her sweet simplicity full oft beguiled
   Him from his books, to rivulets and bowers;
Their merry laughter rang out sweet and wild,
   As each the other crowned with wreaths of flowers:
"Sister," he lowly sighed; she murmured, "Brother:"
And each was all the world unto the other.

XVI.

A lonely girl was the fair ISABEL;
   And solitary seemed her honored sire;
Few were his words—and yet he loved her well—
   Her happiness appeared his great desire:
His voice, like tones of pensive music, fell
   So gently on her ear, it did inspire
For him a filial reverence, so divine,
She could not of her loneliness repine.

XVII.

He made no mention of her childhood home,
   Nor taught her to repeat a Mother's name,
She knew not why he did an exile roam,
   Nor what his sorrows were, nor whence he came:
She only learned that in the time to come,
   There did await her honors, wealth and fame;
That in a sunnier clime beyond the Sea,
They should enjoy serene felicity.

XVIII.

Though, thus the bow of promise, fair and bright,
    Bent o'er the future with celestial gleam;
The past, all shadowy as a restless night,
    Or like the flitting fragment of a dream,
Would rise before her:—one lone ray of light
    Just breaking on oblivion's darksome stream:
A rose-bud, opening on a desert heath;
An infant, smiling in the arms of death.

XIX.

Though ISABEL was yet a child in years,
    Scarce fourteen summers blooming in her face,
Her smiles were sometimes dimmed with anxious tears;
    O'er her soft features thought would often trace
The shadowy line commingling hopes and fears,
    And make the present seem a dreary place:—
A lone oasis smiling on the waste,—
The friendship of ANSELMO—warm and chaste.

XX.

But now drew near the hour when they must part;
    When she must journey with her sire afar;
The tidings, long-expected, made her start,
    And blanch as pallid as a fading star;
Faintness and languor fell upon her heart,
    Her eyes suffused, her nerves were all ajar:
She hastened from her father's presence, lest he
Should seem observant of her misery.

XXI.

In gushing tears she sadly sought relief;
   Tears only made her wish to weep the more;
Slumber, with broken dreams, increased her grief;
   She seemed to wander on a foreign shore,
Far from Anselmo. On a dismal reef,
   The surging billows with wild fury bore
A shattered bark, upon whose quivering prow,
Anselmo stood with dark and troubled brow.

XXII.

And so she moaned the live-long night away,
   Nor thought of love as cause of such distress;
She longed the coming of the tardy day,
   That on Anselmo's bosom she might rest
Her weary head; and, like a child at play,
   Receive, reciprocate his warm caress;
And fondly gazing in his loving eyes,
See her own image dance in fairy skies.

XXIII.

Ah, well-a-day! caresses cure not love:
   She told him all her sorrows; and she wept:
He could not weep—he had no tears to prove
   His love:—at once his youthful spirit leapt
To lofty manhood—in agony he strove
   To quell the mystic power which had slept,
Dreamless, within his heart, but now arose
Majestic from its long and deep repose.

XXIV.

There is a glance of purity, which wakes
    The hallowed flame of love's consuming fire;
There is a touch of tenderness, which makes
    Its object thrill with rapturous desire;
A sigh, which fraught with fervid passion, shakes
    To earth the blossoms which to heaven aspire:
So round the heart of charming ISABEL,
The love-emotions of ANSELMO fell.

XXV.

Love rules the hour! Their hearts dissolve in love,
    And mingle in its dear, delicious dream;
Impassioned sighs their soft affections move;
    Their souls o'erflow with passion's rosy stream;
Their blending thoughts expand and soar above,
    Lighting their eyes with a diviner gleam;
Their spirits glow with love's refining fire,
And quaff the bliss which earth and heaven inspire.

XXVI.

As if entranced with his deep emotion,
    Her brow reflecting heaven's chastened ray,
In the soft, silent rapture of devotion,
    She listened to this half-reproachful lay:
"I wildly drift o'er Love's tumultuous ocean!
    Where is my heart? Ah, whither doth it stray?
Say not, my ISABEL, that we must sever,
Ah, me! thine eyes glow like love's luminous quiver!

XXVII.

"Their heaven-tinted shafts of living fire,
  Pierce through my spirit like ethereal light,
And with warm, deep, insatiate desire,
  Fasten my gaze upon thy ravishing sight!
Oh, turn thine eyes away! Nay, now inspire,
  And crush me with intensely fond delight!
My soul responsive to thy glance of love,
Soars beyond stars—disdaineth thrones above.

XXVIII.

" Thy cheek on mine allays its feverous glow;
  My heart burns, unconsumed with quenchless fire;
Thy balmy kisses so divinely flow,
  My bosom bursts with surges of desire;
Oh, take thy lips from mine! my joys o'erflow—
  I faint with bliss—with rapture I expire!
Nay! Soothe my passions with thy lips' life-balm!
Kiss me into madness! kiss my phrenzy calm!"

XXIX.

Responsive thus:—with young love's artless grace,
  She softly warbled this melodious measure,
Symphonious echoes floating o'er her face,
  Her eyes effulgent with love's liquid pleasure,
Her form to him concentrating all space,
  Her lips yet thrilling with that rapturous pressure,
Love's ruby seal, to Angels never given,
  Blossom of earth, more rich than fruits of Heaven:

A'NSELMO.

1.

In my soul a star is shining,
    Dissipating all its fears:
On thy bosom, now reclining,
    All my passions melt in tears;
Star of beauty! Star of power!
    Far excelling stars above;
Tell me, in this happy hour,
    Art thou not my star of love?

2.

In my heart a fount is springing,
    Limpid, sparkling, bubbling, bright;
Fairy forms around it singing,
    Love is warm and pure as light.
Fount of healing! Fount of pleasure!
    Murmuring through affection's grove;
Thy rich streams, in charmful measure
    Warble, 'tis the fount of love!

3.

Star refulgent, shine forever!
    Make my spirit glow like thine!
Rosy fountain, like a river,
    Flood my soul with joys divine!
Burn within me like devotion,
    Star excelling stars above!
Fountain flow out like an ocean,
    Boundless as eternal love!

XXX.

Brilliant and brief, as on the brow of night
   Gloweth the gleaming meteor's beauteous bloom;
So quick and radiant in its rapid flight,
   The bliss which left their spirits wrapt in gloom:
Ere they had drained the first draughts of delight,
   Their youthful hearts, as with prophetic doom,
Trembled with fancies undefined and fearful,
Till they were silent, sorrowful and tearful.

XXXI.

The crystal streamlet, murmuring through the grove,
   Is more delightsome than its torrent rush,
And more resembling the pure light above
   The cheek's soft glow when fades the ruddy blush:
So, sadness is the luxury of love,
   Of first-love's youngest, warmest, wildest gush:
In love harmoniously all passions move,
And tearful silence is the heaven of love.

XXXII.

The golden Sun, now lingering in the West,
   Transported, shed love's halo all around them;
The feathered warblers sought the shade for rest,
   Erratic with the harmony which bound them;
The flowers sank languid on their mother's breast,
   The earth confess'd the bliss which did surround them:
The balmy eve, love-laden from the skies,
Descending, made the scene a Paradise.

XXXIII.

Oh, love—first-love! how beautiful thou art!
　All things grow lovely in thy loving light:
Thine empire is the universe; the heart,
　The young heart, is the home of thy delight;
There thou dost reign supreme; no guileful art
　Can enter there to breathe its moral blight:
Thou art all trust and truth—to thee is given
Divinest bliss—for where thou art is—Heaven.

XXXIV.

Beneath a maple, branching wide and free—
　The witness of their first full day of love,
Whose branches, tuneful with love's minstrelsy,
　Whose leaves were breathing airs saints might ap-
They bowed together in rapt reverie;　　　[prove—
　Their hands were joined, their eyes were fixed above:
No word was spoken, and no pledge was given—
Their marriage-vow was registered in heaven.

XXXV.

What need of words from lips so warm and true?
　What need of pledge from hearts so fully one?
The air they breathed was love; the twilight hue
　So light with love, they needed not the sun
To cheer their footsteps homeward; early dew,
　Love-lit, like stars, upon their pathway shone:
The parting kiss was given o'er and o'er,
And sanctioned with a thousand kisses more.

XXXVI.

How little did those youthful lovers dream,
　　When thus so lovingly they bade good-night:
The flowery banks of Time's delusive stream [bright;
　　Are strewn with wrecks of hopes—once fair and
Of joys, once rich and warm, and as supreme
　　In all which gives the human heart delight,
As those which all that blissful day came down
From Heaven, their young and holy love to crown.

XXXVII.

A few bright hours: the morning light appears;
　　The scene hath changed: is it a magic spell?
Or, hath she realized her darkest fears?
　　Alas! ANSELMO, loving ISABEL
Hath grief too deep to find relief in tears:
　　She journeys with her father; nor can tell
To him her love; nor how his acts, unspoken,
Have severed two fond hearts, and left them broken.

XXXVIII.

On still she journeys, noting not the time, [years:
　　Save that the days seem weeks, the nights long
She knew not when she reached that sunnier clime,
　　The object once of hopes, but late of fears;
Where youth and beauty spring to life sublime,
　　And move at once in love's more perfect spheres:
Enough to know, that from ANSELMO parted,
Her dreams revealed him wandering, broken-hearted.

XXXIX.

What now were books to him?   Had he not read
   The breathing pages of a human heart?
Of woman's heart?—whose every line doth shed
   A glory science never can impart;
Had traced all passions, to their fountain-head
   Of love-eternal, on this living chart:
His sky, a raging tempest overcast,
His hopes, his joys, were scattered to the blast.

XL.

Lonely and sad, he wandered far away
   From boyhood friendships, beautiful as brief;
On mountain crags, where the wild chamois play;
   On ocean isles, unshaded by a leaf;
In almond groves, where youth and beauty stray,
   He sought allayment for his love and grief:
But found, nor distant sea, nor varying clime,
Hath half the solace of revolving time.

XLI.

Where the proud Hudson the bold highlands laves,
   Sweeping nature's lofty battlements between,
And spreads below in broad and joyous waves,
   Kissing the flowery lawns and groves serene;
There, midst ancestral domicils and graves,
   Despite corroding years, yet staunch and green,
ANSELMO found in friendship's smile and tear,
Rest and relief from travel and from care.

XLII.

The genial quiet of his Hudson home,
    Like dew distilling on the thirsty flower,
To charm him from the restless wish to roam,
    Did promise fair with its beguiling power;
And with the aid of melody and tome,
    And fairy forms in rustic halls and bower,
To win back the young wanderer, and impart
Love's mellow lustre to his way-worn heart.

XLIII.

The boldest projects of the human soul
    Oft burst like bubbles on the rock of fate;
Wise schemes, which would our destiny control,
    A breath of air—a dream—may dissipate:
And he believed in dreams, and that dread scroll
    Necessity rolls up for small and great,
Which sleep unrolls for dreamers to explore,
And light their spirits with prophetic lore.

XLIV.

ANSELMO, in a vision of the night,
    Stood on the summit of a pine-crowned hill;
And, on the smooth sea, slumbering in moonlight,
    Saw pass before him, spirit-like and still,
A form divinely fair—a child of light—
    Whose sea-shell shallop, guided by her will,
Moved o'er the ocean's eddy-dimpling bosom,
Graceful as Nautilus—light as a blossom.

XLV.

Waving her fair right hand, her loose attire
  Disclosed a diamond cross upon her breast:
He knew the sacred charm;· again the fire
  Of love rekindled, with its deep unrest;
Its sweet delirium, and wild desire;
  Its hopes all-wavering, and its fears all blest:
She pointed to the sunny South, and said,
"There shall we meet!"—the blissful vision fled.

XLVI.

Faith, once triumphant, never yields her sway;
  Her children never learn the word—defeat:
ANSELMO rose up with the dawn of day;
  Home and its joys were prostrate at his feet:
The sole companion of his wandering way,
  A harp, though old, yet tremulously sweet,
Which, long responsive to his hope and fear,
Oft soothed his heart, and charmed his tuneful ear.

XLVII.

A mellow morn in June: the springing flowers,
  The emerald grass with dewy diamonds strung,
Danced in the sunbeams; silver-fringed showers
  Skirted the west; Iris, aerial sprung
The Hudson; dreamy kine breathed balmy hours; [sung:
  Flocks gayly frisked; bright birds blithe anthems
Beneath an elm, shading the cottage nigh,
He viewed this scene, and sang this gay good-bye:

ANSELMO.

1.

My gentle harp, we now
　Will join our notes in tuneful lays;
Unwreathe dull care from off our brow,
　And welcome happier days.
What! Tremblest thou with fear?
　Seest thou some lurking danger nigh?
Are joys we leave behind too dear
　To bid them all good-bye?

2.

Ah, what are home and friends,
　When spirits beckon us away
To love-lit shrines, where beauty blends
　Our hope and destiny?
Pale sadness, now depart;
　And thou, my bosom, breathe no sigh;
Now cheerfully, brave, loving heart,
　Bid friends and home good-bye.

3.

My birth-place, thee I greet,
　Thou fairest of Potomac's daughters;
Next loving friends—this dear retreat,
　And Hudson's rolling waters:
My star of destiny,
　Love-blooming lights the southern sky,
And beckons me—so, cheerfully,
　I bid you all good-bye.

4.

My native land, good-bye!
  Fate points me to a foreign shore;
Love's labor wrought, to thee I'll fly,
  And rest me evermore:
On some lone mountain crag,
  Or in thy free, unfathomed wave,
Happy, if but my country's flag
  Float proudly o'er my grave!

XLVIII.

And thus ANSELMO left his highland home,
  And wandered onward to the far sea-side;
Buoyant and blithesome as the lightsome foam
  Bubbling around his foot-prints in the tide;
By love's own inspiration forced to roam,
  He scanned the rolling ocean far and wide,
With the nonchalance of an amateur,
Who dares the storm and mocks its dismal roar.

XLIX

Borne on the pinions of imagination,
  His muse with gleesome exultation flies,
Weaving some golden gossamer creation,
  Finer than earth and fairer than the skies,
But finds no lustre like the corruscation
  Which flasheth forth from lovely woman's eyes;
So soft, effulgent, dazzling, melting, tender—
Who, blest with such an angel, e'er would lend her.

L.

To his confessor? Still less to a sinner,
   Or to his oldest friend, or youngest brother?
For though she were in love a mere beginner,
   Fraught with the lessons of a virtuous mother,
And there should be no effort made to win her,
   Would not her fancy prompt to wound another?
To hurl one shaft of love with soft velocity,
Merely to gratify her curiosity?

LI.

And who would chide her? She alone inspires
   The dullard, man, to deeds of noblest duty;
She kindles in his heart immortal fires;
   Refines his sordid passions for mere booty;
O'erwhelms his soul with joy and warm desires,
   Till at the roseate shrine of love and beauty
Prostrate, he cries—"My undefiled! my dove!
Stay me with flagons; I am sick of love!"

LII.

Woman is the lily which adorns the river;
   A flowering vine, fragrant with ripening cluster;
A fount of living joys, which flow forever;
   A gem of finest ray and purest lustre.
Her love is better far than wine; she never
   Forgives a captive who doth once distrust her:
And woman, too—it may be a mere notion—
Hath much resemblance to the rolling ocean!

LIII.

From old-times to the present, the Atlantic.
　　Like womankind, with various affection
Inspireth voyagers: while some seem antic,
　　Others appear to suffer from dejection;
Some reeling leeward, grow profanely frantic;
　　While all from mutinous stomachs seek protection:
Love-sick, no doubt—what else could so excite them?
So much annoy—so nauseously delight them?

LIV.

A woman's love is shoreless as the ocean;
　　Her peace more calm than ocean's blandest hour;
Far more profound the depths of her devotion:
　　His wrath sublime; hers maketh conquerors cower;
He wrecketh navies in his dark commotion;
　　She crusheth armies in her wanton power.
Alike their bosoms bare, with free translation,
For noblest craft of every age and nation.

LV.

Lonely, amidst a throng at sultry noon,
　　While sadly gazing on the yielding wave,
Wreathing the gallant prow with curls, and soon
　　Subsiding quietly, as doth a slave
Retire, when he with menial hands hath strewn
　　Fresh flowers upon an honored master's grave,
Where gentle ones should scatter every leaf,
And keep them humid with the dews of grief.

LVI.

Low voices whispered: Through life's varying clime,
    Mortals move on as trackless as the wind:
There are no foot-prints on the sea of Time,
    Save the bold imagery of lofty mind;
With rapture soar the souls, whose thoughts sublime,
    The themes of wisdom and of truth unbind;
They revel on the everlasting heights,
Where faith reveals to love its balmiest flights.

LVII.

Thoughtfully musing on familiar scenes,
    Receding fast, full-long—perhaps, for aye:
Weehawken, wrapt in solitude serene;
    Manhattan, empress of the land and sea;
Gowanus, and the Islands gay and green,
    Where ever float the banners of the free,
Till startled memory, like a surging wave,
Portrayed a bridal wreath—a yawning grave.

LVIII.

Repressing symptoms of intense emotion;
    He turns from sorrow's sombre shade away,
And hails with sweet surprise and deep devotion,
    The Narrows merging in the sounding sea:
He hastes to give thee greeting, proud old ocean,
    And glory in thy grand immensity:
Time, like thy tide, from Montauk to the sea,
Rusheth on to mingle with eternity.

LIX.

Chiefly the future wishing to survey,
  His vision oversweepeth ships and shores;
On, on the vista openeth, as the day,
  Broad, brighter, beautiful, until it pours
Brilliance on all things. Surging on his way,
  At sunset, winds were marshalling clouds to wars
Of storms and tempest; flushing, fluttering—
Night soothed thee under her maternal wing.

LX.

Now passionless and placid as above thee,
  In azure beauty blooms the summer sky,
So mellow, languishing, who would not love thee?
  Gloat on thy bosom with lascivious eye?
Thou seemest as if nought could ever move thee
  To wrath—to roll thy billows up on high;
The horizon now so beautifully rounded,
Only by thee, and by the sky is bounded.

LXI.

Poets have sung thy towering wrath sublime;
  Have praised the more sublime magnificence
Of thy majestic calm; in stately rhyme
  Have crowned thee likest to Omnipotence!
These strains were only the far-echoing chime
  Of their fine phrenzy's peerless eloquence,
Rolling through earth and heaven, in lofty numbers,
To waken both spheres from untuneful slumbers.

LXII.

Thou art no emblem of eternity!
   Law mocks thee with a—"thus far shalt thou go!"
Thou art no image of the Deity:
   Unstable! Uncreative! Apropos
Of Godhead—thou hast taint of lunacy?
What dost thou when thy proudest currents flow?
Like a sick swain, whose love retires too soon,
Thou moanest night-long to the wanton moon.

LXIII.

The laughing zephyr wakes thy frowning mood;
   The sportive gale excites thy roaring rage;
The drowsy calm lulleth thy billowy flood
   Thou sport of revelling winds in every age!
Full many a day and night on deck he stood,
   To scan thy breadth, thy boundlessness to gage,
Hoping to find thy realms as broad as day;
Fearing proofs might tear the cherished thought away.

LXIV.

Full soon the land appeared; the bubble broke;
   The blissful vision like a phantom fled;
The grand idea was gone; and he awoke
   From the fond dream with aching heart and head;
His soaring fancy owned the enchanter's stroke,
   And fell, as if from heaven, among the dead!—
'Tis sad to learn the Navigators' line,
Proves thou art neither boundless nor divine.

LXV.

But woman is divine! She lives in love;
   She breathes the breath of immortality;
She walks in beauty; soars where angels rove;
   Blends all the charms of ideality!
Her plastic spirit grasps the bliss above;
   Warms spirit-shades to fond realities!
Her boundless heart proud man can never measure;
Her soul divine pants for immortal pleasure.

LXVI.

But, hist thee, old Atlantic: yonder sun
   Now gloweth on thee as magnificent
As when old Time the march of life begun,
   By leading blushing day before his tent;
When earth, and morn, and man his favor won—
   Doth he not image forth the Omnipotent?
When thou shalt be no more, that sun will be
Man's noblest emblem of the Deity.

LXVII.

Oh, heedless on thou rollest, bounding billow,
   Freighted with blissful joy, and sootheless sorrow:
The gentle bosom which hath been the pillow
   Of one lone heart—which throbs a dark to-morrow—
Now yearns for rest beneath the weeping willow,
   And long ere spring shall come, from grief may borrow
Her dark funereal robe; may feel the pressure
Of that mould-depth, no line of light can measure.

LXVIII.

Away, sad fears: away, all dark foreboding:
    Who can resist a destiny impelling?
Grief brings its own cure in its dull corroding;
    Time hath the gift of mystery-dispelling;
Death will unlade poor mortals of their loading,
    And soothe their sorrows in his silent dwelling:
Restiveness never made the weary stronger,
Nor patience the exhausting journey longer.

LXIX.

See! down the West, voluptuously reclining,
    In tropic beauty, Cuba doth repose:
A bolder outline southwardly defining,
    Jamaica in full vernal glory glows;
Eastward away, like some high-priest divining, [snows,
    Clad in summer's gorgeous vestment fringed like
More proudly than among the Greeks, Achilles—
Riseth fair Hayti, Queen of the Antilles.

LXX.

Three rival kingdoms riseth on the vision;
    Three foreign nations in our own broad seas;
One in their hatred—one in their derision
    Of Freedom's banner floating on the breeze—
Whose Stars shall light the world—heal all division,—
    And guide America's high destinies:
Columbia's constellation, like devotion,
Inspires the free and brave on land and ocean.

LXXI.

Islands of beauty! Isles of the golden West!
   Perennial glory crowns your lofty brows;
For your fair groves Autumn weaves no sombre vest;
   Winter's icy hand plucks not your fruitful boughs;
Spring wantons on your softly-swelling breast,
   And fruitful Summer is your faithful spouse:
The seasons in their course renew your pleasures;
The year rolls round to renovate your treasures.

LXXII.

Grandly emerging from the depths of ocean;
   Symmetrical as heaven-constructed towers;
Your air, the balmy breath of love's emotion;
   Your daughters fairer than their native bowers;—
Well might those sons of God, whose fond devotion
   To earth-born maidens, chose to spend their hours
Of soft dalliance, luscious-lingering kisses,
Mid isles so fair, so redolent of blisses.

LXXIII.

Fair, as when full three centuries gone by,
   Ye wonderingly behold a glorious One,
Clad in the panoply of Earth and Sky,—
   Bearing on his thigh the sword of Arragon—
And in his hand, that emblem from on high,
   The conquering Cross of God's eternal Son:—
Who in the light of Woman's smile, unfurled
The Western skies, and gave her back—a World!

LXXIV.

There was a time—it was when Time was youthful—
    Ere his smooth chin grew dark with rolling ages;
When marts were fair and free, and merchants truthful;
    And man was just, without the rules of sages;
When Law was Right: Theology was sootheful:
    And Physic, like the kiss of maids and pages,
Taken for pleasure, and reciprocated,
To keep the blood cool and unmedicated:—

LXXV.

When blooming Time, in bridal robes attired,
    Led forth the Seasons from primeval bowers;
Gently his right hand blushing Spring inspired,
    While Summer, decked with wreathes of fadeless flow-
Joined hands with fruit-crowned Autumn; all admired [ers,
    How pensive Winter's heart dissolved in showers,
When in his left he drew her right, with cheer,
Forming the mystic circle of the Year:

LXXVI.

Such was the time—a pleasant time, forsooth,
    When down the beatific valleys wended
A noble group of gay and gallant youth,
    Who from the parapets of heaven descended
To see the bliss of Earth—and prove the truth,
    That beauty, life and love in woman blended:
But where they found their soul-enchanting women,
Is yet a problem to divines and seamen.

LXXVII.
Bend to thy swelling canvass, noble Crescent;
  Thoughts of oppression crowd my burning brain;
Where is the yeoman's cot—the free-born peasant?
  Doth man here writhe beneath the galling chain?
The dark inquisitor and thong are present,
  The struggle—and the darker tyrant's reign:
Haste—for though lovelier than the fair Bahamas,
These Eden-islands have been Aceldamas.

LXXVIII.
Faith softly whispers:—yet a little while:
  The day of their redemption draweth nigh;
Power can not stay, nor diplomats beguile
  The quickstep march of their proud destiny;
Fate points the hour when Liberty shall smile
  On these fair sea-girt Isles benignantly;—
And lead them forth in starry robes divine,
To join Columbia's hosts at Freedom's shrine.

LXXIX.
Southward; south-westwardly sublimely sweeping
  Over the jealous Carribean Sea,
Whose restless bosom, like a woman weeping,
  Throbs with a sigh and heaves tumultuously,
When'eer the zephyr, in its embrace sleeping,
  Starts from its couch to join the revelry
Of wanton winds:—Land, ho! The look-out cries,
Under the lee-bow, whither turn all eyes.

LXXX.

To gaze on the horizon: there half-dozing,
  The sky and ocean the strained vision sealeth:
Full soon the main, like a huge cloud reposing
  On evening's verge, the vista half revealeth;
The darker outline of the land disclosing—
  No longer the bold mountain tops concealeth:
Anon, with joy, the quickened eye beholdeth
Granada's beauties, as the mist unfoldeth.

LXXXI.

Behold the Isthmus! The unbroken band
  Of union by which Continents abided:
Is this indeed the far-famed flowery land,
  Which for unnumberered ages hath divided
Two mighty Oceans? On whose pearly strand,
  Their waves have broken, but to be derided?
Darien! All eyes behold thee with much wonder;
How hast thou kept those proud old Oceans under!

LXXXII.

Land of the palm-grove: rich, voluptuous land,
  Forever teeming with fruits rare and mellow;
Thou hast not been defiled by labor's hand;
  Art hath not made thy blushing bowers sallow;
No ruthless axe laid low thy forests grand,
  Nor ploughshare left thy virgin soil fallow:
Spontaneously and in abundant measure,
Thou pourest forth thy stores for food and pleasure.

LXXXIII.

There San Lorenzo, with war's thunders laden,
  High on a rock reposeth midst fair bowers:
Here, gliding Chagres, evermore arrayed in
  The richest garlands of perennial flowers,
Bears on her bosom, like a mountain maiden,
  Bi-ocean mists dissolving in soft showers,
From summits 'neath which Gorgona reposeth,
And cliffs where Cruces the West Sea discloseth.

END OF CANTO I.

ANSELMO.

CANTO SECOND.

I.

The pride of Darien is Panama,
   A city built of yore by brave Castilians,
With massive walls and towers, for peace or war,
   At an expense of unrecorded millions;
A waste of gold, but right enough, so far,
   For they had fleeced the natives of their billions;
They are withal a very pious people,
For every house surmounts a cross, or steeple.

II.

Brave birds bereft of freedom and of beauty,
   Nature's own sentinels of time and love,
Call forth those saints to pleasure, prayer and booty,
   So, throng the pit below, the throne above;
And there is one which doeth constant duty
   For Church and State, more gentle than the dove,
Sad, silent, solemn, smelling for his gizzard,
Dark angel of the city, Turkey Buzzard.

III.

This city occupies a rock plaza,
   An old resort of Buccaneers for playing
Brag; for whose invention Nebuchadnezzar,
   Was doomed to play the ox, and practice praying;
A better fate than had his son, Beltshazzar,
   Who lost his crown, because his guests, obeying
The royal mandate, quaffed their rosy wine,
In goblets pillaged from Jehovah's 'shrine.

IV.

Here commerce is content with narrow streets,
   By overhanging balconies half-shaded;
No ponderous cars unlade her freighted fleets,
   No labor-saving powers are here paraded
Her gold and silver, corn and wine, and meats,
   Go meekly forth on trains of mules, jaded,
Wind-broken, spavined, by turns restive, antic,
To the interior towns and the Atlantic.

V.

Beyond the gates of Panama, reposing,
   Are blooming gardens and perennial groves;
Flowerets and fountains modestly disclosing
   Their varied charms and breathing mutual loves;
Blossoms exuding balmy odors—dozing—
   Dream, while the fluttering humbird sips and roves;
These lull the Wanderer's thoughts to pleasant themes,
And bid his childhood home return in dreams.

VI.

The half-blown flowers shed richer fragrance round;
    The streamlet lingers in the shadowy brake;
The bubbling spring forgets its murmuring sound,
    And zephyrs languish on the slumbering lake;
The herds recline upon the rising ground;
    The birds sigh to each other—half-awake;
Half sleeping in the dreamy twilight bloom,
Till all is hushed in eve's enchanting gloom.

VII.

Charmed with the scene, ANSELMO lingered here,
    Till moonbeams, gleaming through the foliage,
In softly varying shadows, did appear,
    Like the loved idol of his pilgrimage:
Was the form fancy? Real the truant tear,
    Kindly refractive medium to assuage,
By fond illusions his unsolaced grief,
Which sought no sympathy, asked no relief.

VIII.

And yet, it may not have been fancy, all—
    This land was ISABELLA's childhood home;
That sunnier clime, o'er which, in dreams a pall,
    Like cloudlets breaking o'er a luminous dome,
Or, waiving mist above a water-fall,
    Seemed hanging ever; hither had she come,
Obedient to the mandates of her sire,
To garner honors sought not with desire.

IX.

Here she had found position, wealth and name;
    The goal and glory of her sainted sire,
Who scarcely had resumed his ancient fame,
    Ere, in his daughter's arms, he did expire:
Alone, earth's joys and pride were poor and tame;
    They could not in her striken heart inspire
That deep, abiding bliss which those inherit,
Whose cherished longings soothe the wounded spirit.

X.

Here in the cloister's consecrated shade,
    Away from the disturbing themes of earth,
Where fashion's froward throngs dare not invade,
    Nor come distractive revelry and mirth,
Her soul a pious offering she made,
    Renounced the world, her name, and pride of birth;
With vestal virgins counted all things dross—
She found the consolations of the Cross.

XI.

Her heart was now a fountain of repose,
    Whose pure depths shadowed forth the beautiful
Of earth and heaven: her early love and woes,
    Commingling, merged; while in the dutiful,
Her spirit seemed absorbed; divinely flows
    The well of living waters, deep and full,
Free from the taint of earth, its pride, its strife,
Springing joyous up to everlasting life.

XII.

Charmed with this blest, religious quietude,
   Time glided peacefully without alarm;
The softened scenery of the solitude,
   Gave her fair features a more heavenly charm;
She passed serenely into womanhood—
   She thought no evil, so she feared no harm:
Her struggle with the world long since had ended—
Anselmo's image with the Savior's blended.

XIII.

A mother may forget her darling boy,
   A wife forget the husband of her youth,
But the blest image, drawn with guileless joy,
   Of girl-hood's first love, like eternal truth,
Fades not: absent her mind may find employ
   In sacred rites, but her fond heart, forsooth,
Throbbeth in worship as if he were near,
And would with rapture leap should he appear.

XIV.

In day-dreams oft, and visions of the night,
   There comes a music fraught with sweet repose,
Which to the yearning spirit gives delight,
   As to the dew upon the opening rose,
When rifting fragrance lets in hallowed light,
   And in its exhalation doth disclose
Those beauties which withstand the ardent spell
Of noontide glow—so came to Isabel

XV.

The voice of one whose name she did repeat
   At matins and at vespers, quite as oft
As to a sacred vestal it were meet,
   In rich melodious intonations, soft
And low as fairy foot-falls in retreat;
   Then rose a radiant halo, as aloft,
A luminous cloudlet heralding a storm,
Revealing to her gaze ANSELMO's form.

XVI.

Oh, vision blest! In meditations sweet,
   She mused along the windings of the shore;
A dove from seaward fluttered at her feet,
   On its fair neck a golden chain it wore,
Whence, delicately set, with art replete,
   In diamonds, hung ANSELMO's minature;
She kissed the weary wanderer to her breast,
Where saints might slumber, angels sink to rest;

XVII.

More white and warm, more soft than eider-down,
   Purer than sunbeams chastened through eclipse,
The carrier nestled gently, deeply down
   Twixt lily pillows with carnation tips;—
Fit throne to wake the envy of a crown,
   Dreamily sipping opiates from her lips;
Awhile in rest—and then, as if inspired,
It breathed one note of joyance and expired.

XVIII.

The moon now sinks behind yon hill forlorn,
  Whose bold outline falls dimly on the sight;
The fleeting smiles of the awakening morn
  Scarce tinge the silvery sheen of starry night;
Love's lilies fade when passion's blush is born,
  So fadeth now the retinue of night:
Ray fuseth ray, and gleam suffuseth gleam,
Till dawn's soft twilight reigns o'er all supreme.

XIX.

Day, like a youth of tireless energy,
  Riseth up from the banquet halls of Night;
Jocund with joy, refreshed with revelry,
  Shakes from his broad brow looming into light,
The wreath of cloud-rifts, which, with exstacy
  The goddess Storm had decked him for his flight;
Earthward he glanceth a full quickening ray—
Dim twilight disappears and all is gray;

XX.

Gray as yon graveyard walls, with cells so narrow,
  Each can admit one shrouded tenant only;
There the ancestors' bones scarce yield their marrow,
  Before the heir usurps the place, so lonely,
Dark, putrid, reeking—vile enough to harrow
  The soul of any being, save man only;
Out goes the Father's carcase, scarce half-rotten,
To make room for the Son, long since forgotten.

XXI.

This is a sort of special abdication,
  Not of a throne, but of a marble palace;
A gravely kind of pious abnegation,
  Which might atone for much paternal malice;
The index of a passing generation,   [chalice;
  Whose lips no more shall touch the wine-crowned
Whose voice no more shall cheer the festive board
In praise of lovely woman—and the sword.

XXII.

Where now is he who skilfully and bold,
  Built yonder highway grappling fast two oceans?
Now broken, rugged, rocky, rough and old,
  Inspiring pilgrims with profane emotions,
Over which hath passed, of silver and of gold,
  Enough to rouse a world's sublime devotions;
Sleepeth he there, unknown to partial fame,
Without a tablet and without a name?

XXIII.

And where is he who built yon city walls,
  Combining science, beauty, strength and skill?
Whose lofty towers, and broad and spacious halls,
  And spires with symbols of peace and good will;
Designs, the missing draughtsman oft recalls;
  Structures survive the bold constructive will:
The still corroding power of Time appals
The bravest hearts—even Rome in ruin falls.

XXIV.

From Art, and her proud monuments, away
    We turn, to gaze on Nature's lovelier face:
And while up yonder mountain-paths we stray,
    With light heart and firm footstep, let us trace
The everlasting hills—the beauteous Bay—
    Expanding with sweet majesty and grace;—
Her bosom swelling with divine emotion,
To join the solemn matins of the Ocean.

XXV.

Cerro de Ancon! On thy brow of pride
    Effulgent with the smiles of glowing Day
Bloometh the ruddy Morn—a blushing bride—
    Uprising, joyful, from the snowy spray;
Her rosy fingers gently put aside
    The fleecy folds of gorgeous drapery,
With which the Tropics robe the Orient portals,
Whence comes the Day-good—brightest of immortals.

XXVI.

The Sun looks forth from Ocean! Glorious Sun!
    Exhaustless source of rich and pure delights:
To hymn thy praises, countless Planets run
    Their endless rounds of glory! Father of lights!
Beauty is thine! And Life! And Love! Triune:
    Unchangeable: invariable: the heights
Which bear aloft the everlasting throne
Are not more firm than is thy power alone.

XXVII.

Hail! glorious Bridegroom of the Universe;
  Magnificent in all thy goings forth;
Earth's renovator from the primal curse;
  Thine Eunuchs are, the East, West South and North:
To whom the Twelve continually rehearse,
  In brilliant signs the Zodiac of thy worth!
When with the Morning Stars thou didst rejoice,
Eternity resounded with thy voice.

XXVIII.

A slumbering world awakes to greet thee now:
  Earth, from the mystical abyss of Night,
Looms gayly forth, like some tall, gallant prow—
  Grace in her motion; in her face delight;
Hope, joy and love illume her noble brow;
  Her emerald robes with diamond dew-drops bright;
Sweep lightly o'er her high diurnal course,
And raptly sing thine all-attractive force.

XXIX.

Now the Pacific leads the choir alone:
  Mountains in chorus bow their reverend heads;
The palm-crowned hills waft incense to thy throne;
  Rivers glide joyful o'er their golden beds:
Toboga, 'mid green isles—a fairy zone—
  Daily thy morn-beams bride-like blushing weds:
And fair Losaria, glittering with the hues
Of brilliant birds, thy morning praise renews. |

XXX.

From sleep yon city starts with new life given;
  Luxuriant vales with fragrant bliss opprest,
And flowers excelling the rich hues of heaven
  Spring, childlike, forth to thy paternal breast;
And yon dark forest, by fierce Art unriven,
  In deep and solemn tones proclaims thee blest!—
Viego Panama! Ruin's hoary son!
Even thou dost smiling greet the rising Sun!

XXXI.

But, yonder solitude awakens not;
  Thy beams light not the shrouded tenants there;
Of earth forgetful, and by man forgot,
  They praise not thee, nor heed thy grand career—
But thou shalt see Death, vanquished, fly that spot:
  The Dead come forth! the Master re-appear!
The Temple rise, immortal in design;
Praise thou, oh, Sun, the Architect Divine.

XXXII.

Here might one linger till life's sands were run,
  Alike forgetful of Earth's love and hate;
But wherefore leave a chosen task undone?
  Why should the Morning on the Evening wait?
Up and pursue thy course, like yonder sun;
  Work is the charm which foils the shafts of fate;
Though faint, press on, broken shall be the spell,
Anselmo, which still shrouds thy Isabel.

XXXIII.

Descending from DeAncon's glowing height,
   In a cool grot, o'erlooking town and bay,
He saw an ancient man, whose brow of light
   And eye of love, a minstrel might portray,
Who bade him welcome with that frank delight,
   Which from a stranger takes reserve away:
Anselmo sat beneath the flowering vine,
And shared the minstrel's mellow fruit and wine.

XXXIV.

They soon are friends, and soon the converse grows
   To themes of love, so genial to all poets:
They drink, and tell the tales which each best knows,
   And what's untold, the other longs to know it;
At length the native minstrel's heart o'erflows,
   He doth confess himself Don Carlos' Poet;
To please his guest, with mingled grief and pleasure,
He sings his Patron—thus the song and measure:

XXXV.

Hispania, Father-land of Panama,
   By home-bred discord long was rent asunder;
Peace fled her cheerful vales, and civil war,
   Wrapt in dark, gory robes and crowned with thunder—
Like avalanches rushing from afar—
   Her iron heels crushed men and cities under
Vast smouldering heaps of undistinguished ruin,
Ere the Panamians knew the storm was brewing.

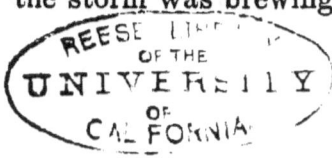

XXXVI.

O'er hill and dale, in palace, cot and tower,
    From Murcia's vale to Malladetta's summit,
From dreamy dawn to drowsy midnight hour,
    Chiefs raised the war-cry, warriors did hum it;
Of Spain's proud chivalry went forth the flower,
    To fire and thrust and cut, to fife and drum it:
Being without foreign foes, but of game mother,
With pious zeal each good Don fought his brother.

XXXVII.

Don Carlos heard these tidings with a presage
    Of sorrow, like a shadow undefinable
Flitting 'thwart his brow; flashes of fear and rage,
    To which his heart a moment seemed inclinable;
Brave Saul, the Witch of Endor did engage,
    To try for him her arts and skill divinable:
Heroes who dare War's iron-bolted thunder,
To a small spirit-voice oft knock under.

XXXVIII.

The noble Don awhile did hesitate
    What course events demanded to be taken;
And though opprest by some dim shade of fate,
    His towering soul vile fear had never shaken;
He gave in his adhesion to the State,
    Whose glory his ancestry had partaken:
Thus, love-paternal bowed to royalty,
The purest pledge of spotless loyalty.

XXXIX.

His patriot spirit glowed with martial fire;
    He fought again the fields he won of yore;
Ambition might not bolder hopes inspire,
    Nor haughty fame on loftier pinions soar:
Now burning with an impulse deeper, higher,
    The crown to his liege sovereign to restore;
Or, midst the grape and canister's dead rattle,
Fall like a hero foremost in the battle.

XL.

Once, when red slaughter drunk with blood, had driven
    The carnage on from fields to walls and towers—
War's thunder-bolts the massive gates had riven,
    And deluged hearths and homes in sanguine showers,
Don Carlos saved—was it the will of Heaven?—
    An orphan from the ruin which devours
Wife, child and sire—as his own son did rear him,
And for the sacred mitre did prepare him.

XLI.

The Don's chief care, such as a father feeleth,
    Was for the welfare of his fledgling dove;
How great the confidence when doubt ne'er stealeth
    In, as we yield the treasures of our love,
To whom even gratitude and honor sealeth
    Our friend below, our guide to joys above?
He made Juan guardian of his house and daughter;
And left his home for distant fields of slaughter.

XLII.

The Dona Julia was the holiest treasure,
   Her princely, widowed father had on earth;
He celebrated with unbounded measure,
   The bright May-day which gave his daughter birth.
To her devoted all his hours of leisure,
   And found in her a child of peerless worth;
All praised her as the beau-ideal of beauty;
Her life was the embodiment of duty.

XLIII.

Scarce thirteen summers, with unwonted fleetness,
   Had wafted her through vales of thornless roses;
Infused her ruby lips with tropic sweetness,
   Balmy as the bosom on which Love reposes;
Her eyes revealed a soul of perfect meetness,
   For spirits who inhabit where day closes
Its lingering, hallowed glance on things terrestrial,
And melts away in starry light celestial.

XLIV.

She loved the beautiful: the clouds and showers;
   The early beam, whose radiant kiss unsealeth
The eye of morn; those richly-fragrant bowers
   Where noon-tide's glow a chastened gleam revealeth;
Young dew-drops nestling on her favorite flowers;
   The bow—which Heaven's promise ever sealeth,
Zephyrs sporting with the pensive shades of even,
And stars dissolving in the light of Heaven.

XLV.

She loved the beautiful: the grace of motion;
　The tuneful lightning trilling on the air;
The eagle soaring sunward with devotion;
　The noble form of manhood, strong and fair;
Diviner woman—radiant with emotion,
　When love hath plucked from passion its despair,
Thought, like an Angel, on the brow reclining,
The wonders of the Universe divining.

LXVI.

She loved the beautiful: not merely beauty
　Of hue, form, motion; thought, high, deep and broad;
More beautiful to her the path of duty,
　Where Meekness, Mercy, Truth divinely trod;
She saw, admired, adored the moral beauty
　Which bindeth Angels to the throne of God!
More beautiful, more hallowed the emotion
With which the Cross inspired her devotion!

XLVII.

The soothful warmth of passion's virgin kiss;
　The blossom breathing fragrance to the dove;
The dream foreshadowing joys of future bliss;
　The echo murmuring to the tone of love;
The ray uniting heavenly worlds to this;
　The gleam transporting earthly thoughts above;—
These join all kindred souls in sweet communion;
These Julia cherished in life-giving union.

XLVIII.

Well might Don Carlos' proud and lofty spirit,
    Rejoice with all a father's holiest joy,
In this fond daughter, whose angel's merit,
    Was far too pure a source of bliss to cloy;—
His sole blest gift of Heaven to inherit
    Name, virtues, glories, Time might scarce destroy:
The breath polluting so divine a blossom,
More rots itself than rends a father's bosom.

XLIX.

The name of Guardian implieth duty;
    And duty joineth hands with obligation;
Both may prove true against mere sordid booty,
    And even turn the edge of gratification;
But flesh and blood ne'er yet resisted beauty,
    However smooth the age, or rude the nation;
It ne'er was in the power of nomenclature,
To change the current of frail human nature.

L.

Saint, guardian—bishop, words of magic power,
    As ever made poor mortals lay the lash on—
Are far less potent than an April shower
    To quench the fervid flames of youthful passion;
Vain words to sap the old Adamic tower—
    In spite of them, young blood will ever dash on
Its fiery course, resistless as the ocean,
While every billow breaks with soft emotion.

LI.

That heaven hath its favorites none can doubt,
    And doth allow to some, what it denies
Unto the race; the general rule found out;
    As this—"The Soul that sinneth surely dies,"
Implies exceptions: hence the elect devout
    May very many naughty things devise:
Like Jacob, when among his Uncle's kye,
Placed hazel-rods to charm their lustful eye.

LII.

So David, the man after God's own heart;
    Who dared Goliah forth to mortal strife;
Who swept the tuneful lyre with heavenly art;
    Whose sacred numbers breathed eternal life,
And still to saints doth joys divine impart:—
    This godly prince seduced Uria's wife,
Then made him drunk and slew him—laid the offense
On the devouring sword and—Providence.

LIII.

Look not upon the wine when it is red;
    When it doth sparkle like a living thing;
For when it cheers the heart and warms the head,
    It biteth like a serpent; and its sting
Is like the adder's:—thus, with pious dread,
    Did Solomon unto his neighbors sing;
Then called a brand of father Noah's time,
And drank nine healths to dusky Ashtorime.

LIV.

Solomon was an exception to all rules;
  Rich, learned, pious, powerful and wise;
He said much in his proverbs about fools,
  Which yet in preaching wisdom vast implies:
A generous man; no tyro of the schools;
  In passion's contests always won the prize:
To all the sex, devoutly did impart,
In tender tones, the gushings of his heart.

LV.

Woman was to him the poetry of life;
  The soul subduing eloquence of earth;
And whether it was concubine or wife,
  Her winsome smile afforded equal mirth.
No creed, no color, gave him cause for strife;
  He loved the sex for their intrinsic worth:
Thus, one rule hath philosopher and lover—
Woman is woman all the wide-world over.

LVI.

Yet, saint-like, he did piously condemn
  Adultery, and such like naughty things,
In scathing tirades which might overwhelm
  A harpy crew, despite their loathsome wings:
In Hebrew ribaldry and holy phlegm,
  Abused the sex, the chief delight of kings—
A fair translation of which to repeat,
Would make this page to modest eyes unmeet.

LVII.

Nor Jew alone, but his more modern brother,
    The Christian—grinds the face of all God's poor;
He sells a pious child, a godly mother,
    Just as a Pagan selleth a wild boar;
He loves this world, believeth in the other;
    Prays for the slave, and driveth from his door
The beggared orphans of his kith and kin,
As if to aid white sufferers were a sin.

LVIII.

Thus, every man is right in his own eyes;
    A yielding faith is a most blessed thing;
He who for Heaven on his good works relies,
    Had better when he is a dying, cling
To his old hope, as at the sacrifice,
    A bullock doth unto the butcher's ring.
Like Juan, the saints enjoy Earth's pleasures more
Than promised joys on Heaven's distant shore.

LIX.

The Bishop-Guardian was so young and gentle;
    So blandly pious and so meekly handsome;
His manners, features, glance so sentimental,
    A maiden's heart might innocently dance some
In his sweet smile—yet find it detrimental;
    If long enjoyed, demanding ransom:
But ransom, though full, fleet and disenthralling—
Can ne'er erase the stain—for guilt is galling.

LX.

How could she doubt him? He, who oft had shriven
    The father, on whose love and worth she doted:
Could he prove false to whom she had been given,
    To teach her holy themes of the devoted?
To guide her in the narrow path to Heaven?
    She did not dream a Bishop so much noted
For self-denying zeal in things celestial,
Drank daily deeper draughts from springs terrestrial.

LXI.

Juan was a man of polished education;
    Highly accomplished for a lady's tutor;
Classic in composition and translation;
    But rather warm and gallant to be neuter,
When he might choose t'wixt nought and recreation;
    He proved himself a charming teacher-suitor;
Giving at noon-tide, vespers, dewy-matin,
Alternate lessons of Greek, Love and Latin.

LXII.

A sacerdotal devotee of pleasure;
    His diocesan duties were regarded,
As better suited for the sacred leisure,
    Of prayerful priests, who seek to be rewarded
With spirit-bliss, as free from sense as measure;
    But for himself, he thought to be retarded
In earthly joys like those which grace a bridal,
Was spurning heaven's gifts by being suicidal.

LXIII.

Fruits fairest, smoothest, mellowest and roundest,
    He could enjoy in all sorts of weather;
Of theologian Sages he was soundest,
    His theory and practice went together;
Philosophy, said he, is the profoundest,
    Which freeth nature from all legal tether:
Fastings for Monks; for Bishops sumptuous dinners;
Free grace for Saints; the Law for Jews and sinners.

LXIV.

'Tis said, Priests prate of sin with holy horror;
    Toward common sinners show but little lenience;
Condemning that to-day, which on the morrow
    They do themselves, nor think of penitence:
They may not wed, though oft, 'tis said, they borrow
    A layman's spouse, as matter of convenience;
Imparting thus a sanctifying flavor;
To keep the common salt from losing savor.

LXV.

This may be so: the Priesthood are but mortal;
    And mortals are of compounds the most curious:
Creatures in whom dame nature queerly wrought all
    Virtues and vices, mildest and most furious:
Strange clouds of darkness tinged with light immortal;
    Genuine in evil; in all goodness spurious:
Crosier, nor cowl, nor coat of rigid Quaker,
Can curb the passions given by our Maker.

LXVI.

Juan was much like his prototype of old,
   Who when he heard, in Eden there did dwell,
A lovely being of diviner mould,
   Whose sunny smile and laughing eyes could tell
A tale of wondrous love; whose charms did hold
   Even angels by a supernatural spell;—
Whose merry laughter floating on the wind,
The heart enchanted and enrapt the mind:—

LXVII.

His gallant spirit caught the genial flame;
   His heart with passion's ardor beat once more;
Up to our earthly paradise he came,—
   Milton hath told us how he left the shore
Of Erebus: in strangely happy frame
   He gazed on Eve, and gazing did adore;
Adoring loved, and loving raved away,
Like gay Lotharios who on virtue prey.

LXVIII.

That fruit is dangerous, who can disbelieve?
   Though how, or wherefore, few may understand:
Sathanus knew it when he tempted Eve,
   Saying, as he placed the apple in her hand,
Eat; be like God, and never die! Believe;
   Eat! be immortal in thy beauty; and,
Their hands touched; did their lips? Woman's first sigh
Doth often seal her future destiny.

LXIX.

The hand is a machine of wondrous power;
   It sweepeth ancient temples from the earth;
Where yawns the abyss, it rears the stately tower;
   To solitudes it giveth cities birth:
It is surcharged with strange electric power,
   Which thrilleth woman's heart with pleasant mirth:
Hand toucheth hand, the heart vibrateth free;
All love, but who can solve the mystery?

LXX.

Ripe lips are love's galvanic battery—
   As they approach the heavenly sparks appear;
Till with their touch, the quick intensity
   Of flame dissolves the heart into a tear.
Immortal kisses! Heavenly ecstacy!
   This was the youthful Bishop's daily prayer—
Though Heaven deny me every other pleasure,
Let me forever feel their magic pressure.

LXXI.

Man plucks the blooming rose with grateful pleasure,
   And breathes its fragrance when its beauty fadeth;
But casts away, as counterfeited treasure,
   The flowers immortal which his lust degradeth:
Illicit joy hath neither shame nor measure,
   In blasted hopes and broken hearts it tradeth;
Forever planting thorns, where bloometh roses;
Its dreams are deepest where foul death reposes.

LXXII.

The ills of life crowd fast upon each other;
   Woe presseth hard upon the steps of sadness:
The hour which crowned Julia as a mother,
   Forever sealed to her the fount of gladness:
He who in trust should have excelled a brother,
   Consigned her to cells of corroding madness:
To kill, and not be tyrant, or magician,
Power needs but to employ a bland physician.

LXXIII.

Such was the Quadroon Bolus, who delighted
   In guise of friendship, to inflict oppression;
To work dark deeds against his honor plighted;
   His blandest smiles were falsehoods in succession:
His words infection which fair virtue blighted;—
   A titled member of the grave profession,
Who make their art subservient to their passion,
And gloze the villany time-honored fashion.

LXXIV.

Such was the one to whom was fitly given
   The genial task of Julia's full destruction:
He bled—to mend a heart by anguish riven,
   And smiling, showed it Galen's best instruction;
Blistered—to cure a mind to madness driven,
   And aptly proved it right by book construction:
Weak, timid, fallen, thus he briefly wrote,
"Light is your bane—darkness your antidote."

LXXV.

Bright rose the morn—the patient rose in gloom;
    He found her waiting him with bandaged eyes;
He smiled with pitiless triumph o'er her doom,
    And with low voice he softly bade her rise;
Gently he led her to her living tomb,
    Where never came the light of mellow skies;
Kissed her a fond adieu: his work was done,
Just where the jailor Kaznoe's task began.

LXXVI.

This Kaznoe was of obscure foreign birth;
    The protege of a dark courtezan;
A vile creation of course, filthy earth;
    Odors of Africa betrayed the man;
His only pleasure was polluting worth;
    He was chief panderer to the Bishop Juan:
A braggart, coward, stealthy in his blows;
Alike a traitor to his friends and foes.

LXXVII.

Don Manuel's parentage was deemed uncertain;
    The Bishop Juan first saw the pretty child
In the Cathedral, near the silver-curtain
    Which veiled the Virgin, whose fine charms beguiled
Him many an hour, from duties which did pertain
    To heavenly things; for he believed she smiled,
Whene'er he knelt before her: to Faith is given,
The power to change the love of Earth to Heaven.

LXXVIII.

He should have recognized the little stranger
    At the first glance: for in its tiny features,
Blended his own so fully, there was danger,
    If any of the world's inquisitive creatures
Should see its face, they would not seek a manger
    To find its father: on the tropic sea-shores,
Sinners and saints, and priests and virgins bathing,
Avoid the heats of purgatorial scathing.

LXXIX.

The holy man was shocked to find a new born
    Babe, sleeping near the altar of the Dove;
But soon his heart, with strange emotions torn,
    Leap't toward the infant with paternal love!
"A Pope in embryo"—he would have sworn,
    But as he spoke, a whisper from above
Said, sprinkle the dear child with holy water—
Devote it to the Church as her own—Daughter.

LXXX.

Juan's heart sank fast below the range of zero;
    His priestly spirit rose divinely high;
And glancing upward, amiably as Nero
    When fiddling over Rome, his ear and eye
Caught a soft foot-fall moving to and fro,
    And a fair vestal figure drawing nigh;
The step, the form, the hour he knew full well,
Proclaimed the Lady Abbess, Rosabel.

ANSELMO

LXXXI.

Surprised, but not confused, devoutly kneeling,
    Juan held the infant in his arms, and prayed;
Most holy Virgin! Inspire, with kind feeling,
    The Lady Abbess to regard this maid;
Found quite forlorn beneath this sacred ceiling;
    May she, thy favorite, with thy heavenly aid,
Rear this lone one to happiness divine,
That, like herself, it grow a saint of thine.

LXXXII.

Fair Rosabel at once knelt down beside him,
    Full as devoutly as the holy father;
Suspicious—that she knelt there to deride him,
    With dark, unkindly glance he did regard her;
But wise as kind, she did not even chide him—
    She bit her lips to keep from laughing harder
Than it is meet a saint should at the altar—
His features tinged as though he felt a halter.

LXXXIII.

Closing his eyes, a rueful prayer to mutter,
    He fancied on his lips a humid pressure;
His goodly heart began to beat and flutter,
    As when it throbbed the first impulse of pleasure:
"Divinest!" Not a word more could he utter;
    Her pleasantries flowed with unwonted measure:
Oh, woman! thy devotion is a fountain;
Thy love an ocean, and thy wit a mountain.

LXXXIV.

Woman is a book, whose fair, mysterious cover
   Displays to all the golden clasp of love;
Revealing, as time turns its pages over,
   The rose and lily, olive-leaf and dove;
And, yielding to the pressure of the lover,
   Imparteth blissful joys unknown above:
Rich incense, grateful as a rose-wrought column,
Involves the student of this mystic volume.

LXXXV.

A book, whose pages are so plainly written,
   That he who runs may read: still it is thought,
That many an old fox has been sorely bitten,
   When he believed young maiden geese were caught:
Only a noble heart can be love-smitten—
   A woman's heart can not be sold, or bought:
She, like a diamond, there writes secrets deeper,
And safer keeps them than a conscience-keeper.

LXXXVI.

Love hath its trophies among saints and sinners,
   Alike, in every age, in every clime;
How little of its power know new beginners;
   Love hath, like woman, its resistless prime:
Excelling all the love of mutual winners,
   Its prayer, hope, fear, its sighing, trysting-time:
Love's legal joys are wife and sons and daughters;
Life's rarest essence is love-stolen waters.

LXXXVII.

Occasion makes the man, man makes occasion;
   And each unmakes the other quite as often;
But woman hath the power to make evasion
   Frank as the truth, with gentler warmth to soften;
She never is the victim of occasion;
   She bends events; if necessary, coughs when
She may not speak, nor hear the word, which spoken,
Would leave her fond lord's heart quite rudely broken.

LXXXVIII.

Oh love! Thou art a theorem to man;
   To woman, a plain problem of pure pleasure;
Which oft she solves to prove creation's plan
   Both wise and good, of boundless zest and measure:
To her, eternal life is pleasure's span;
   Glory, the gem of fond desire's treasure;
She jilts a lover with a playful nod,
And, smiling, spurns an Angel, or a God.

LXXXIX.

But Man, the doating dullard, vainly dreams,
   That love is intellectual and divine;
A zone of lofty thoughts and holy themes;
   A fadeless wreath, faith, hope and virtue twine;
A diamond, glowing with celestial gleam;
   Star of that sphere where truth forever shines;
Poor victim of fond woman's fascination;
He knows love only by—anticipation.

XC.

A sacred Boudoir: here the Virgin smiles
   With beatific radiance on her Son;
There the young noble Nazarene beguiles
   Mary of Magdala, the loveliest one
Of lovely women: spotless, undefiled,
   A dove descending 'mid soft cloudlets shone:
There Lebanon—and there the Temple glows;
Below, blest Kedron murmuringly flows.

XCI.

A clustering vine around the lattice strays,
   Breathing fragrance over Cana's marriage feast;
Near Sychar's well, a shaded fountain plays;
   Sherbets, wines, fruits invite the coyish taste:
Rich, drowsy perfumes lade the visual rays,
   And sofa's strewn with flowers invite to rest;
A Bishop analyzing Sharon's rose—
An Abbess in voluptuous repose.

XCII.

The chainless hours in their rapid flight,
   Heed not the mandates of plethoric leisure;
They scorn the pride and power of wealth and might,
   Nor linger 'midst the shades of luscious pleasure;
On their broad, tireless pinions day and night,
   They bear away the unestimated treasure
Of life's exhausted moments to their Giver,
To be returned again—no more, forever.

XCIII.

So fled the hour, the dear delicious hour,
    Which Bishop Juan for many a month had given,
As a restorative of moral power,
    To lady Rosabel, and love and Heaven:
Refreshed, as dews revive the drooping flower,
    He said, "My heart with pitying grace is riven."
Rosabel replied, "Alas! poor broken-hearted,
Give me the child:"—then saint-like she departed.

XCIV.

The youthful Nun to whom the Abbess gave
    The new-born babe, for an inheritance,
Was one whose beauty smote, but ne'er would save
    Her numerous victims from love's penitence;
With smile and kiss, she conquered gay and grave,
    And bound them with her soul-enchanting glance:
But musing once along a flowery dale,
She, slipping—soiled her ringlets—took the veil.

XCV.

Instead of fading like a half-blown flower,
    Whose petals perish in the breath of even,
As may have been designed; a gorgeous bower,
    Warm shade and mellow sunbeams could have given
The boy no attribute of lovely power
    Which clustered not around him: rainbows riven
By angel glances, shed not richer hues,
Than Time o'er his fine features did diffuse.

XCVI.

Time is a fair, fine, fat and jovial fellow,
    Forever sporting with the human race;
Full oft he makes the blushing maiden sallow,
    Blends rose and lily in some younger face;
Ripens the dimpling mouth and cheeks, so mellow,—
    They melt between our lips like love and grace:
He lavisheth on man both strength and beauty;—
Then stops his breath—as a mere act of duty.

XCVII.

Fast fly the moments to a hungry man,
    When he sits down to eat a sumptuous dinner;
Quickly the hours dwindle to a span,
    When playeth deep the bold and reckless winner;
Long nights of pleasure scarcely seem began,
    When dawn breaks in on a young rollicking sinner:
So swiftly fled seven golden cycles annual,
To fair Anita and her love—Don Manuel.

XCVIII.

Her love! Anita dearly loved the child,
    Yes—she adored her blue-eyed beauteous boy;
She loved her girl-boy with a passionate, wild,
    Consuming, deep and overwhelming joy:
His presence all the ills of life beguiled;
    His absence all life's blisses did destroy:
He was to her, son, daughter, sister, brother—
Her only love in this world—or the other.

XCIX.

Love springs spontaneous from the soul's deep fountain;
    Pure as the stream of life's pellucid river;
Wells upward to the spirit's loftiest mountain,
    Thence through the heart pours its fond tide forever!
What mortal can the flood immortal contain?
    Why flows it back to life's eternal Giver?
Love's sigh excels a seraph's rapt emotion:
Love's gushing stream is an eternal ocean.

C.

The Minstrel paused: a fitting time for rest:
    The tropic noon with stealthy lassitude,
The body and the mind alike opprest;
    While mother earth her breast with flowers strewed,
To the siesta welcomed host and guest;
    Now while they slumber, let us not intrude,
Nor judge too harshly of the Minstrel's song,
Lest he should not his chosen theme prolong.

END OF CANTO II.

ANSELMO.

CANTO THIRD.

I.

Not long the Minstrel slept. His thoughts refused
   To sink at bidding, to profound repose;
They had been marshalled to a theme unused
   For many a year; and now they would dispose
Of it. His mind a moment seemed confused
   With various themes: at length the Minstrel rose;
Tuning his harp, he swept its chords again,
And thus renewed the song with solemn strain.

II.

Life, overflowing its eternal fount,
   Exultant down the everlasting skies,
In crystal streams, too numerous to recount,
   Too complicate of form to analyze,
Flooded the rude, dark earth, o'er vale and mount,
   Till out of chaos, order did arise:
Light shed o'er the abyss its soft effulgence,
And beauty, smiling, dallied with indulgence.

III.

The grass sprang wanton from earth's quickened breast,
  Robing its parent in immortal green;
And balmy herb, and fragrant flower imprest
  The verdant vesture, with celestial sheen;
And trees full grown, leapt forth from their long rest
  Flinging umbrageous branches o'er the scene:
While bud and blossom grace the clustering vine;
And blushing fruits with mellow radiance shine.

IV.

Forth from the teeming depths of ocean came
  Gigantic forms of animated being;
From rivers, finny tribes, web-footed game,
  Surprise themselves with swimming, flying, seeing;
And birds of richest hue and ardent flame,
  Vocalize the grove with passion's charmful gleeing;
Gay flocks, grave herds range, happy o'er the plains;
The lion, monarch of the forest, reigns.

V.

Then Man stood forth; the noblest form of life;
  Extreme of fancy and reality;
With tameless appetites and passions rife,
  And lofty intellectuality;
Blending with peace the elements of strife;
  Mortal conjoined with immortality;
Alone, he stood! Creation's lordly head,
Unblest, unmatched, unmated and unwed.

VI.

To charm his loneliness, with sweet surprise,
   Laden with golden fruits and fairest flowers,
Eden sprang forth to his admiring eyes,
   Replete with murmuring streams and fairy bowers,
He saw the Tree of Life immortal rise,
   To nerve with angel strength his mortal powers;
Fountains of bliss—full soon insipid grown;
He slept—all solitary as the Sun.

VII.

Satiate with sensuous bliss, he soundly slept
   Beneath the shadows of life's balmy tree;
And sleeping, dreamed; and dreaming, sighed and wept;
   But whether sighs of joy and tears of glee;
Or, griefful thrilling o'er his spirit crept,
   Remaineth yet a darksome mystery:
He slept, unconscious that his sporting side
Had lost a rib, or won for him a bride.

VIII.

Up-borne, self-buoyant, wandering—he dreamed:
   Far, far away beside a silvery river,
With wreaths of rose-buds crowned, he saw what seemed
   A man in miniature, with bow and quiver;—
For on his virgin fancy ne'er had beamed
   The idea of a Boy! Nor would it ever,
Had not a tiny shaft that moment prest
Its wounding point against his naked breast.

IX.

A lily-leaf-boat floated from the shore;
 Away wafts Cupid down the limpid stream,
His merry heart with laughter runneth o'er;
 His wanton eyes with Love's soft malice beam:
The wandering dreamer finds surprising more,
 Each new-wrought feature of his pristine dream:
Smiling, he plucks the Lilliputian's dart;
Sighing, he feels its point hath touched his heart.

X.

See, on his mossy couch, inlaid with flowers,
 With changeful brow, how restlessly he turns;
The lights and shadows glow and fade, like hours;
 Conflicting passion in his bosom burns;
His soul seems wrestling with superior powers;
 His heart accepts the bribe his spirit spurns:
He would be chief of an immortal race;
Not the joint limner of an infant face.

XI.

He wakes: his lips are thrilling with a kiss!
 From ripe lips, rich as wine and pure as fire:
Woman the glorious bribe! The sum of bliss!
 Inhales the flames her beauty doth inspire:
Raptly, he cries, what new-wrought joy is this?
 His eyes gleam love through mists of soft desire:
With love's refluent tides, her heart opprest—
Languid—she sinks on the same couch to rest.

XII.

Oh, sleep! Thou art indeed a wondrous thing—
    More wonderful the dreams thou dost inspire;
The earth-born sense dissolves: on bouyant wing,
    The disenthralled spirit mounteth higher;
Drinketh deep draughts from life's reviving spring;
    Gloweth with beams of love and thoughts of fire:
Sleep gives the weary rest, the wanderer hope;
Dreams are the soul's divine kaleidoscope.

XIII.

What fate ordains, 'tis madness to oppose;
    Folly to scan the dark decrees of Heaven:
Dream on, fond pair! Ah, brief is your repose;
    Bitter the draught of life to mortals given,
Ere thrice yon sun his annual round shall close,
    From your sweet paradise ye shall be driven,
By Cherubim, now eager for the strife;
Armed with the sword, to guard the Tree of Life.

XIV.

The sword! Ah, that reminds me of my theme:
    The sword was forged in heaven by hands divine;
The free and brave admire its vivid gleam;
    The fair, with flowers, its lustre doth entwine;
When myrtle-wreathed, 'tis pleasant as a dream;
    Gentle as woman; delicate as wine:
When from the inglorious scabbard it doth leap,
Thrones sink in dust and tyrants basely sleep.

XV.

Don Carlos girded on the trusty sword
  His noble sires had worn in days of yore;
With firm step trod again the rich green-sward,
  Where victory wooed him on his native shore;
But now she gave him a coquette's reward;
  His victories few, his well-fought battles more:
Than foreign war, he found more irksome far,
The household butchery of civil war.

XVI.

Oft-times amid the sanguine battle-strife,
  The proud old warrior felt an intense yearning
To grace the tomb of his long sainted wife
  With tear-libations: homeward he returning,
Would clasp again her image, in whose life
  And love he lived, and kept forever burning
Upon the altar of his heart, the fire
Of nuptial bliss her charms did erst inspire.

XVII.

While thus this noble patriot did exile
  Himself from all the gracious ties which bind
A father to endearments without guile,
  To serve his country when her sons, with blind
Ambition, sought her honors to defile;
  To drive her as a wreck before the wind;
The bishop-guardian revelled day and night;
And found in sensual joys his chief delight.

XVIII.

He had two boon companions, young and gay,
    Who, like himself, were devotees of pleasure:
Don Ramon and Don Tomas; yet, were they
    In creed most orthodox; they laid up treasure
In heaven—by proxy—a convenient way;
    All three were men of letters, lust and leisure:
Being thus congenial, whether wise or mad,—
They called themselves the Philosophic Triad.

XIX.

Their council-chamber was not square, or round;
    It was triangular—the panels three;
Each panel a large mirror, draped around
    With scarlet, purple and white taffeta,
Set with three golden stars on silver ground;
    On the blue ceiling were three ships at sea;
Whence three large lamps, by golden chains suspended,
Thro' shades red, green and blue their soft light blended.

XX.

The altar-table was a central fixture,
    Three-sided, with a finely-polished surface,—
Slate, marble, quartz, in equal parts its texture;
    Two gods, one goddess, did its centre grace,—
The metal,—a brass, gold and silver mixture;
    They stood there back to back, not face to face:
Their names—none need inquire about their genus—
Are Bacchus, Cupid and his mother Venus.

XXI.

A gallon was each god's capacity;
   But each supplied a different kind of wine;
Bacchus, rich port; Cupid, with audacity,
   Mixed with his sherry, a very little fine
Old cognac; Venus, with more sagacity,
   Expressed her champagne sparkling from the vine:
Three golden goblets on the altar stood,
One for each member of the brotherhood.

XXII.

On the rich Turkish carpet was inwrought,
   Most skilfully, three scenes from Scripture taken:
Here, Jacob at the well, his uncle sought;
   Kiss'd Rachel, and then wept, like one forsaken:
There Sampson in Delilah's lap was caught;
   Lot's Daughter's in the cave their father waking:
Those pictures of an ancient pious nation,
Were, to the Triad, food for meditation.

XXIII.

Three seats adapted to the altar sides,
   Not moveable, but of most antique style,
Each seat for one, or three arranged, besides,
   When pleasure did the occupants beguile,
They were extended by a secret slide,
   That weary worshipers might rest awhile;
Between them and the mirrors and each seat,
Were aisles—and other accommodations meet.

XXIV.

The only motto which this temple graced,
    Was taken from the proverbs of a sage,
And was in Latin, Greek and Hebrew traced
    On each bright mirror, as upon a page,—
"Eat drink and be merry"—but why this taste
    For style and learning of a Scripture age?
Surely not for show; perhaps, designed alone,
To give the temple a high moral tone.

XXV.

The rules were three: First; no one shall defile
    The temple with apparel, coarse or fine:
Next; twice three nymphs, the tedium to beguile,—
    The number present must be three, or nine:
Third; open with three rounds in mystic style,—
    And close with three times three:—adding, in fine,
A song from each grave Triad, as doxology,—
And this comprised their wisdom and theology.

XXVI.

In form, the divan opened at eleven;
    And regularly closed at 3 A. M.;
And when the intermediate hours were given,
    By the Cathedral clock, then all of them
Rose up and drank in honor of the Seven
    Wise men of Greece,—and babe of Bethlehem:
On the occasion which is here related,
Ramon sung thus,—to close, as has been stated:

1.

Come let us drink; the midnight hour,
    Invites us all to one glass more:
The toast—confusion to all power;
    Death to all tyrants evermore.
'Tis one o'clock, love's witching hour
    Murmurs the watchword,—one glass more:
The toast;—alone to woman's power,
    We bow in reverence, we adore.

2.

Tis two o'clock: the hour of duty
    Remindeth us of one glass more:
The toast;—a health to love and beauty;—
    Come let us drink it o'er and o'er.
The clock strikes three; the closing hour,
    Invites to three times three rounds more;
The toast;—may we all find the bower
Of Love, upon the other shore.

XXVI.

Then three full rounds were drank by all the nine,
    The first to Bacchus and his royal Port;
The second round to Cupid and his fine
    Old Sherry—mixed with some of stronger sort:
The third to Venus and her sparkling wine,—
    Rich smooth Champagne from distant islands brought;
And as all now were feeling somewhat mellow,
Don Tomas sung like a fine, jovial fellow:—

1.

Oh, let us love, while love we may,
   The morn of life is flying,
And, like the flowers, we pass away,
   Fading, unfragrant, dying.
The early dawn is blithe and gay;
   The spring with beauty gloweth;
But when the spring has passed away,
   And Summer,—then it snoweth.

2.

Oh, let us love, while love we may;
   The thrush loves while he singeth:
In youth the heart with melody,
   And love's own music ringeth.
The tender passions love to play,
   While Time with us is merry,
While dimpling cheeks the rose display
   And lips out-blush the cherry.

3.

Oh, let us love, while love we may,
   Ere care, hope's chalice dasheth;
While yet our eye, the lightning ray
   Of warm desire flasheth;
Like Time, love hath its blooming May,
   All fragrant, sweet, but flying;
Then let us wing its hours away
   With kisses, smiles and sighing.

4.

Youth is the time to love, and they
  Who wait a better season,
Will find that Cupid can not play
  With old gray-headed Reason.
Then let us love, while love we may,
  The morn of life is flying;
And like the flowers, we pass away,
  Fading, unfragrant, dying.

XXVIII.

The second round was drank in gleeful mood;—
  Each Triad held his goblet high, and swore
His own lips should not taste the rosy flood,
  Which sparkled on the dazzling brim, before
The nymphs so fair, which then beside him stood,
  With kisses hallowed it: thus men adore
Women and wine,—whether peasant, priest or king:—
The Bishop now this closing song did sing:

1.

Three in one, now the Triad address,
  As one spirit, the beautiful six:
The new wine which on earth we express,
  We will drink when we cross over Styx.
Wreathe the goblet with roses, my girl;
  Let it sparkle with wine to the brim;
First: a health to old Time, lest the churl,
  Make the soft light of desire burn dim.

2.

Fill to Bacchus, my beautiful girl;
  Let us drink to the clustering vine,
Whose fond tendrils so gracefully curl
  Round the soft swelling fountains of wine.
Fill to Cupid, my loveable girl;—
  The Boy-God and Venus his mother!
Love and beauty! Life's diamond and pearl:—
  And now we will drink to each other.

3.

To thine eyes, my adorable girl;
  Thy ripe lips where smiles wantonly rove:
Stars and rosebuds! I drink while I whirl
  In the wildest delirium of love!
Fill again,—three times three—my fond girl;
  To the silent and shadowy shore,—
All of Earth and of Heaven, I hurl!
  Lip to lip: let us drink evermore!—

XXIX.

Kneeling; each Triad on the altar placed
  His brimming goblet; then beside him knelt
Too charming nymphs, whose youth and beauty graced
  This mystic scene: whate'er was thought, or felt,
No word was spoken: on no brow was traced
  A line of care; all passions seemed to melt
In one broad, calm, deep fount of flowing blisses;—
The rounds thus taken, were surcharged with kisses.

XXX.

Rumor hath wings as potent as her tongue,
  Silent, invisible, mysterious;
To whose remorseless flapping doth belong
  The power to make the giddiest maiden serious:
While man, of bolder spirit, grave and strong,
  By its suspense hath oft been made delirious:
He sees no shadow, heareth no rude sound,
Yet feels the quakings of a fear profound.

XXXI.

Immeasurable space hath not the power
  To stay dark Rumor in her mystic course;
Nor thrones, nor charms of past, or present hour
  Can turn aside her desolating force;
Alike she makes the girl and hero cower,
  Like children in the presence of a corse:
No arrow gleameth through the yielding air;
Still poisoned shafts are falling fast and near.

XXXII.

A broken thought whirled through the Don's head, oh,
  It was mere nothing, still it was unpleasant;
As when a cloudlet flitteth thwart the meadow,
  While yet the new moon is a pallid cresent,
Casting a tremulously doubtful shadow,
  More like the ghostly past than lusty present;
The fragment of a fancy so uncertain,
The Don first thought he saw it through a curtain.

XXXIII.

Full oft it came, and did as often borrow
    A varying shade and form of less distinctness;
Now like a presage of a dark to-morrow,
    Blending the future with a bold succinctness;
Then it would shed a mist of present sorrow,
    So lightly evanescent, he would think less
Of it as a disturber of to-day's rest,—
Than of to-morrow's or of by-gone days blest.

XXXIV.

At length the Don, just ready to depart,
    His proud ship riding by her bower anchor,
Learnt, what the busy world knew long by heart,
    The utter failure of his Bishop-banker:
A subtle pang coiled round his festering heart;
    Which, vulture-like, fed on the growing canker:
As all his thoughts intently fixed upon her,
The winds were whispering Julia and dishonor.

XXXV.

He turned around, like one who makes a blunder,
    To see what curious eyes were fixed upon him;
Or, one who fancieth he heareth thunder;
    Or, what's the same, a voice which doth dun him,
And doubts if 'tis above, or rolls from under,
    As either sphere claims equal right to stun him:
The waves were rolling and the sun still shining,
Poor Tray whose toes he trod on, sadly whining.

ANSELMO.

XXXVI.

No oath was heard, no angry demonstration,
    No furious outburst of controlless passion:
No cursing the Creator, or Creation,
    As with some baptized braggarts is the fashion:
His nostrils showed a little more dilation;
    His color faded slightly to Circassian;
Biting his lips, he kept some vagrant thought in,
Which strove to 'scape the agony it wrought in.

XXXVII.

The good Don was no worshipper of Mammon,
    Nor too devout at any other shrine;
He breakfasted on salad, sack and salmon;
    On oysters, garlic, turkies, trout could dine;
Take his siesta, then chess and back-gammon;
    All hours suited for his Rhenish wine:
With music, dance and song beguiled the even,
Enough for earth, he asked no more for heaven.

XXXVIII.

The spell of silence finally was broken;
    For silence never yet was long in power;
A gentle word, though still more gently spoken,
    Doth thrill it as a touch the sentient flower:
Heaven hath not given to man a single token,
    That it shall reign on earth more than one hour
In Heaven, half an hour is its limit,
Thus proving fewer men than women it it.

XXXIX.

The spell was broken: mildly as the even
   Glides in the dark embraces of the night,
His tone so sad, a heart it might have riven;
   His word betrayed nor passion, nor delight:
"Alas, poor Tray!—have I unkindly driven
   Thee to complain, so faithful, true and right:"
Turning upon his heel, he went awhile thence;
The thought was wrapt in everlasting silence.

XL.

Full many a day the noble Tarantula,
   Swung at her moorings in the bay of Cadiz;
The Captain thought the Don had turned fool, or,
   What he deemed worse, had gone to see the ladies;
He knew not that the only land of Beulah
   The Don thought of, was on the field where grade is
Synonomous with duty, danger, dying;
Triumph pressing forward, foeman flying.

XLI.

On went the Don, through city, town and villa;
   Forward he spurred, of food and horse-hide reckless;
Through field and forest, up and down the hill, or,
   Where rolling rivers rushed on bridgless, deckless;
Ne'er rode more recklessly the wild guerrilla,
   To save his life, or kiss his lady's necklace:
For robber though he be, the smile of woman,
Is dearer to him than the gold of foeman.

XLII.

Old Seville was a charger of great merit;
  His master's spirit he could well divine;
Bucephalus did not more grace inherit,
  Nor bear more safely martial sacks of wine;
Alike they shared their hero's princely spirit,
  And loved the rich dew of the clustering vine:
Seville well knew that when the Don did reel,
His brains were settling down into his heel.

XLIII.

On from the sea-board, as he felt the reins,
  Thrown loosely on his neck by his superior,
He took his way: in titles, not in brains,
  Horses to heroes only are inferior;
He, like a pioneer, swept hills and plains,
  And travelled many a league in the interior;—
He had his own way, like a pretty woman,
Unguided by a hand divine or human.

XLIV.

Night came apace, and Seville yet was flying,
  Heedless alike of substance and of shadow;
Nor when the pallid stars of morn were dying
  Away in light, like lovers growing sadder,
Had his pace slackened, as if he were trying
  His skill at travel, without crib, or meadow:
A patent homeopathic way to fat you;—
Still on him sat Don Carlos like a statue.

XLV.

Neither turned to the right hand, or the left,
    Nor gave to aught the glances of recognizance,
Till down a hill careering, quite bereft
    Of arms and officers, a rout's advance
Were scattering far and wide all things of heft,
    To quicken pace, Seville, with snort and prance,
Dashed from the strange and medley throng away,
And roused Don Carlos from his lethargy.

XLVI.

Don Carlos gazed around, like one awaking
    From a dim dream, devoid of light and gladness;
As one by one his unreefed thoughts were shaking
    In reason's breath, his features gathered sadness;
Then yielding to a fierce internal quaking,
    His brow grew darker with the gloom of madness:
On, Seville, on, he cried; haste thee to slaughter;
Old charger, hist! The watchword is—My Daughter!

XLVII.

Gazing beyond, then in his stirrups rising,
    He stood erect, as if to think a minute;
Not to complete a scheme of new devising,
    But to determine where he should begin it;
Then bending forward, as if still surmising,
    Said—"I have found it; onward, we shall win it:
On, Seville, to the pass of yonder mountain;
We'll turn the tide of war, or drain life's fountain."

XLVIII.

Highway and field, both far and wide are thronged;
   Men, horses, cattle, all in wild confusion;
To whom nor fear, nor cowardice belonged
   Before, were victims of affright's delusion;
Each trode the other down, as if he wronged
   Himself, if he did not inflict contusion
On his next friend, in every step advancing,—
Like politicians 'twixt two parties dancing.

XLIX.

On as they swept, the Don and his black charger,
   Confusion more confounded seized the rout;
The phantom made their fear and courage larger,
   They would not go on, could not turn about;
And though sans powder, shot, sword, musket, targe, or
   Other arms offensive, they were devout
In kicks, cuffs, curses, gratis on each other;
As wealthy christians greet a beggar brother.

L.

The pass is gained: an army slow advancing,
   With arms reversed and colors in the dust,
In sullen gloom, reflecting the mischancing
   Of fields well-planned, far more than a distrust
Of skill, and tact, and bravery enhancing
   The worth of captains; learning as all must,
The battle is not always to the strongest;
Nor wifedom to her who may court the longest.

LI.

On as they march, unheeding all about them,
    Each weary footstep shows them sore distrest, [them
Weighed down with cares more in them than without
    With conscious want of self-respect opprest,
A sturdy warrior's eye would never doubt them,
    Though still retreating, as of nobler crest:
The brave, retreating, lift scarce foot or eye;
Cowards wing their heels, and without blushing fly.

LII.

On still they come; the heavy martial clangor
    Of arms, men, horses, deaden every sound:
Life's in the onset, in the repulse languor;
    All nature suffers with the soul's rebound:
Was that a spirit's voice which just rang? or
    Cometh it echoing upward from the ground?
Cliff answereth cliff, and rocks respond to bowers;
"Halt! Spaniards, wheel! The victory shall be ours."

LIII.

The voice was recognized: their favorite chief,
    Who oft had led them on to victory,
Now came with ample forces for relief,
    Or, now rebuked them from his rest on high:
In either case, the power of belief
    Was strong enough to make them turn and die;
Or, conquer on the field, whence they were driven,
Thus sharing in his triumph, or his heaven.

LIV.

The die was cast: as if by inspiration,
    They flung their trailing banners to the sky;
The fire of war burst from its concentration
    Within, while flitting flames flashed from the eye;
On swept the Don, as if a revelation
    Had been embodied and sent from on high,
To save the Crown, the Cross, the holy Mother,
Inspiring brother saints to kill each other.

LV.

On swept the Don, from line to line, reviivng
    The flagging spirits of the true and brave;
On where the bold, the battle's brunt surviving,
    Still face the foe, not hoping life to save,
But cover a retreat; now backward driving
    The victors to a soldier's gory grave;
Now in their turn, driven to the gates of death,
Backward they enter—like heroes yield their breath.

LVI.

Old Seville, pausing, lifts his head on high;
    Surveys the field with more delight than wonder;
Fierce lightnings flash out from his rolling eye;
    He paws the valley clods and rocks asunder:
Majestic as the tempest-riven sky,
    His proud neck wreathes with rifts of living thunder:
His broad distended nostrils proudly gleaming,
With glory terrible as Ætna streaming.

LVII.

He laugheth at affright: mocks at all fear:
  Deeming the cannon's roar but infant prattle;
Rejoiceth in his strength, as if to dare
  The God of war; the mighty shock of battle:
Leapeth up from earth, and poising mid air,
  Shakes his huge mane, makes the vast concave rattle;
In his own powers placing firm reliance,
Neighing, he hurls the gauntlet of defiance.

LVIII.

Now snuffing up the battle from afar,
  He scents the thunder of the Captain's scouting:
Dashing through bristling files, nor shield, nor spear,
  Rattling against him give a moment's doubting:
To loudest blast of trumpet, cries, Ha! Ha! [shouting
  Sweeps through the serried ranks where wildest
And fiercest fighting flings war's fiery fever
Deep in the veins, exhausting life forever.

LIX.

Fierce is the struggle 'twixt hope and despair;
  More fiercely grapple hope and hope reviving:
Hope strikes to conquer, despair but to dare
  The conquerer to deeds of over-striving,
Who, self-exhausted, findeth false as fair,
  The dead-sea fruits of victory surviving;
Like coquette's triumphs, yet who would restrict her,
The blow which conquers oft exhausts the victor.

LX.

Now lost in dust and smoke; now seen afar,
    Where on the verge of victory, too confiding,
Defeat in darkness sits; oft, like a star
    Gleaming through clouds, the struggling foe dividing,
Don Carlos shone a glowing god of war,
    Contending for the triumph, yet abiding
'Mid fiercest conflict of increasing slaughter;
His only words, "Ho, Seville—hist, my Daughter!"

LXI.

The clash of arms, as brigade and division
    Wheel-in to share the long and doubtful contest;
The groan-rent air; the din of huge collision;
    Rifle balls riddling through the human breast;
The crash of living bones, as with precision,
    Canister and grape, long colunms sweep to rest:
War's glorious terrors in the conflict blending;
Nor with the daylight the death-struggle ending.

LXII.

Terrific War! Whence thy strange fascination?
    Kings play, enchanted, at thy bloody game;
Princes tread thy sanguine courts for recreation;
    Heroes adore thee as the god of fame:
Soldiers, the living bulwarks of their nation,
    Find thy proud triumphs but an empty name;
On them Ambition bids thy legions charge;
Havoc and Death the quivering breach enlarge.

H*

LVIII.

War, what is right? The power to enforce
   On weaker tribes the dictates of thy will?
War, what is honor? A soul where dark remorse,
   Haunts not the hero who hath nerve to kill?
War, what is glory? Carnage in full course
   On Victory's wings, proclaimed by clarions shrill?
Are these thine Ethics? This the glorious code,
By which thou marshallest nations home to God?

LXIV.

Hast thou the warrant of antiquity,
   Endorsed by Reason and by Revelation?
Fire, flood and famine, with prolixity,
   Full often decimate a peaceful nation:
Disease, with powers of ubiquity,
   Devours the human race without cessation:
Are these the harvest implements of Heaven,
To garner up the life to mortals given?

LXV.

War plumes a haughty crest, claims heavenly birth;
   His pride and pomp are themes of ancient story;
Magnificent in madness and in mirth,
   Beauty craves his smile, although his hand is gory.
War sprang not from the pedigrees of earth;
   He rose resplendent in empyrean glory:
And though by Fate, from high Olympus driven,
He dared the Thunderer in his native Heaven.

LXVI.

Erst, in the ancient days of Amraphel,
  When Kings were Patriarchs, and Shepherds Kings;
When marshalled hosts in Siddim fought and fell,
  And victors bore the spoils on vulture wings;
War called the faithful Hebrew to expel
  The proud invaders and bring back Lot's things;
With war-crowned glory, Father Abraham stood,
The foe of tyrants and the Friend of God.

LXVII.

Next on the plains of Troy, in proud array,
  With martial music and bright banners flying,
War, in the cause of Virtue, did display,
  For ten long years, chaste Greeks and Trojans dying!
The gods themselves joined in the grand affray!
  Who could resist the lovely Helen's sighing?
All-glorious War? Though in defense of fillies,
Thou dost create great Hectors and Achilles!

LXVIII.

Whose hand but thine, all terrible and gory,
  Could to the wandering sons of God have given
The pleasant land of Canaan? Whence the glory
  Of Israel, for ages, shown from Heaven.
Moses had in the wilderness grown hoary;
  The Canaanites must from their homes be driven:
Thou did'st beguile the moon in Ajalon,
To crown the victories pious Joshua won!

LIX.

War hath been famous as a politician;
  Most popular in all the generations;
An able and most eloquent logician—
  Severe and mighty arbiter of nations;
Bound to no party, like a bold magician,
  He finds delight in change of place and station:
To-day War crowneth Kings with pomp and glory;
To-morrow blots them from the page of story.

LXX.

War is a most devout Religionist!
  Proselyte and Apostle of all creeds;
Champion of Christian, Jew and Atheist;
  Impartial both to colors and to breeds;
For Romanist, for rigid Calvinist,
  For one and all, War, like a martyr bleeds;
Pouring at every shrine a rich libation
Of blood, to bring poor sinners to salvation.

LXXI.

When through the Orient gross Idolatry
  Reared reeking shrines alike for prince and peasant;
Wrapping, in moral darkness, bond and free,
  Blending the past and future in the present;
War, to the line laid Justice righteously,
  And Judgment to the plummet, by the Crescent;
War crowned with victories the Moslem Prophet,
To save the Nations from the pit of Tophet.

LXXII

When Infidels profaned the hallowed grave
  Of his great rival, Jesus, Prince of Peace,
War, doffed the Crescent, donned the Cross, to save
  The Holy Sepulchre for Rome and Greece!
Made hermits, heroes; timid women, brave;
  And crowned Godfrey in the Holy Place:
War, like a bold and sanctified Crusader,
From Zion hurled the Islamite invader!

LXXIII.

What, if War doth indulge in freaks of slaughter,
  And slake his thirst in seas of human gore?
As, when at Cannæ blood flowed free as water;
  And over Issus like a flood did pour:
Must not the noblest son and fairest daughter
  Of Adam, by Death reach the shadowy shore?
If War had not doomed hosts by Styx to wander,
Where would be Hannibal? where Alexander?

LXXIV.

No mighty Cæsar e'er had graced the world,
  Or made immortal rippling Rubicon;
No thrones of tyrants to the dust been hurled;
  No gallic Eagles—no Napoleon;
Freedom's stars and stripes had never been unfurled;
  Columbia ne'er had known her Washington,
Had War not crowned himself with deathful thunder,
And in warm blood have trodden nations under!

LXXV.

Night wrapt herself in clouds, huge, wild and bleak,
    Drowning the cannon's roar in rolling thunder,
Lightnings flashed forth, as if the very crack
    Of doom had rent the dark abyss asunder,
And let the kindling fires of day come back,
    To help Don Carlos bring the rebels under:
The vivid flash his noble form revealing,
Sublimer than the storm his triumph sealing.

LXXVI.

Fame sketched the field: with heaps of slain all gory;
    The war did with that stormy night expire;
Around the loyal dead gleamed rays of glory;
    Don Carlos' name Fame on her scroll wrote higher;
The poet laureate sang the heroic story;
    His royal patrons did the song admire:
But from these things, Don Carlos could not borrow
A healing balm for his corroding sorrow.

LXXVII.

But Time came to his aid: Time, whom we bless,
    As friend and guardian of our hapless race:
With joy Time brings us love's divine caress;
    Wreathes smiles around the lines care doth trace:
Soothes and sustains our hearts when woes oppress;
    Smoothes the rude scar, death only can efface;
When shaft and wound resist all skill and cure;
Time gives counter joys, and patience to endure.

LXXVIII.

Swiftly the winged seasons passed away;
    Don Carlos wed a young and blooming bride;
His noble ship now fully under weigh,
    Bears them on homeward, with fair wind and tide;
And while on Ocean's wave, yet many a day,
    With joys increasing, they securely glide,—
As the lone watcher waits the tardy morn,
So shall I wait, to welcome his return.

LXXIX.

The weary day adown the glowing West
    Sank on his fleecy couch of burnished gold,
And like the day, the Minstrel needed rest:
    Though young in heart, his harp and hands were old:
He leaned a moment on ANSELMO's breast:—
    The Minstrel's song was sung! His tale was told.
In warm embrace they did awhile remain;
Then parted, pledging oft to meet again.

LXXX.

ANSELMO mused on all the Minstrel sung;
    He mourned the sadness of fair Julia's fate;
While o'er his spirit, like a dark cloud hung
    A feeling of disgust and mingled hate,
Towards the perfidious Juan. War's clarion rung
    Its changes on his ear till it grew late.
He thought of Man's unnumbered woes,—and wept;
He thought of God's unbounded love,—and slept.

ANSELMO.

CANTO FOURTH.

I.

Glide on, thou viewless tide, resistless Time;
　Flow ceaseless on, deep, silent, bridgeless stream;
Sweeping ever on to that mysterious clime,—
　Alike the mighty works and fleeting dreams
Of bouyant youth and manhood's noblest prime,
　Where dark oblivion, undisturbed by beams
Of burning suns, or passion's humid light,
Lulls souls to rest in dreamless realms of night.

II.

The eye, whose piercing gaze, with subtle glance,
　Scans boldly the expanse of earth and heaven,
Hath never seen Thee! Nor thy mystic dance
　Been by the delicate ear, to which is given
Exquisite sound, detected! Thy still advance
　Over hosts of human hearts, by anguish riven,
And crumbling empires, is more silent far,
Than faint rays falling from the loftiest star.

III.

Nor human skill, whose genius spans with ease
    Broad rivers,—and with winged ships and steam,
Bridges the rolling depths of ancient seas,
    And makes the distant shores of Ocean seem
So near—a shallop in a morning breeze
    Might waft across the Atlantic's trackless stream,—
Hath ever spanned thy tide of woe and bliss;
Or pierced the depths of thy profound abyss.

IV.

Oh, bear me onward to my destiny;
    My sad soul flutters like a weary bird;
Corroding thoughts on my lorn spirit prey;
    My heart grows sick with hope too long deferred;
Fancies of youth are fading fast away,
    And young love's dream appears a vision blurred:
Ah, whither shall I roam? What charm dispel
The cloud which veils from me my ISABEL?

V.

Sweet memories, o'er my gloomy spirit shine;
    Bring back the fragrance of love's balmy breeze,
When in her smile, so radiant and divine,
    My soul exulted! On passion's stormy seas,
Where hopes are wrecked, desires oft decline,
    We hailed in signs of love's sublime degrees:
Each found a haven in the other's heart,—
Moorings more safe than rituals impart.

VI.

Hope sprang not full fledged from the eternal sire;
  Nor sang with morning stars at the creation:
Her light burns not with that Promethean fire,
  Which soars divinely from each dire prostration.
Hope is the wanton offspring of desire,
  Warmed into life by fulsome expectation:
Earth-born, Time bounds the circle of its flight;
Death seals the visions of her seerful sight.

VII.

In life's bland morn, Hope lingereth by the side
  Of trustful youth, with smiles of seeming joy;
Sheddeth soft halo over Time's dark tide;
  With golden hues infuseth dull alloy;
Tingeth with glory passion's bliss and pride,
  Bubbles of beauty, faintest sighs destroy;
Then leaves the tyro midst increasing cares,
To rise and wing his flight of future years.

VIII.

In the full glow of life's unclouded noon,
  With firmer footstep and exalted mien,
Manhood surmounts Time's towering steep, and soon
  Scans the wide world with confidence serene,
Till gathering clouds obscure sun, stars and moon,—
  Then cometh Hope with her delusive sheen,
Luring him 'midst ambition's bold, dark mountains,
To drink deep draughts from folly's bitter fountains.

IX.

When deepening shadows lengthen o'er life's strand,
    And Age doth totter with the weight of years,
Slowly, wearily toward the spirit land,
    Which bounds the welkin of this vale of tears,
The Pilgrim lifts his staff with trembling hand;—
    Steps falteringly amid more darksome fears:
Expecting Hope's bland smile to light his way,
He sinks in gloom unriven by a ray.

X.

Hope's last faint glimmer gone, huge shadows dark,
    And death-mists the lone Pilgrim overwhelm:
See,—yonder onward sweeps his sea-worn bark;
    He droops exhausted o'er the guideless helm;
Black, broken waves, emitting not one spark,
    Fast-driving, sweeps him to that unknown realm,
Where dim Fate shrouds each solitary guest;
Whence none return to tell us they are blest.

XI.

Hope,—fond illusion, which forever hovereth
    Over the dark and devious paths of mortals,
Lighting with flickering ray the shade which covereth
    Life's everlasting high and holy portals;
From whose soft lures, the pilgrim ne'er recovereth,
    Till death reveals the land of the immortals,
On the far side of that dark, rolling river,
Which sweeps away all human hopes forever.

XII.

So darkly endeth all our mortal woes;
    Thus all our earthly joys must terminate;
The way-worn Pilgrim only finds repose
    Through Death's indefinable cloudy gate:
Faith, hope, love, hate, desert him as he goes
    Alone, to learn his own mysterious fate:
Doth Man there like a wandering spirit rave?
Or sleepeth he beneath oblivion's wave?

XIII.

Thus, on a cloudless summer morn, afar
    From the turmoil of human habitations,
Amidst the ruins of old Panama,
    Where Flora wantons with blear Desolation,—
From a watch-tower, whose broken front might mar
    Even Melancholy's evening meditations,
ANSELMO mused, as with intense emotion,—
Scanning the smooth expanse of slumbering Ocean,

XIV.

He saw a gallant ship, like an outline,
    Drawn by some Angel hand against the sky,
Rise on the far horizon's azure line,
    With swelling sails and tall masts tapering high;
Saw faces glowing with a hope divine,—
    Hope, full of promise to the ear and eye:
Heard merry voices ring with grateful glee,
For having 'scaped the dangers of the sea.

XV.

Swiftly a huge cloud overcasts the sky;
  No thunder wakes the elements to war;
One bright bolt bursts in silence from on high,—
  Writhing she reels;—she sinks! Above the roar
Of billows one wail breaks! The storm-clouds fly
  Exultant back to the dark stygian shore:
The winds were hushed: the waves slept dreamlessly,
As those they shrouded in the deep blue sea.

XVI.

Oh, 'tis a mockery all—this thing of life;
  The jest of Time; the sport of elements;
Earth-born, it wasteth with perpetual strife,
  The soul corrodes itself and tenement;
The air we breath with atom death is rife;
  Waters quench its flames with taunting merriment;
Hope trifles with the savage and the sage;
Time grinds to dust mankind in every age.

XVII.

A biting jester was that Hebrew Seer,
  Who saw the image of the God-head shine
On the pale brows of that fond mortal pair,
  Who dwelt in Eden of the auld lang syne:
Eternal glories crown a thing of air?
  Base metal coined with a stamp divine?
He proved Life's jest;—on Jordan's desert side,
From Nebo saw the promised land—and died.

XVIII.

While yet strange shadows cloud ANSELMO's brow;
    Unconsciously he hastens to the strand;
In fancy sees the brave bark's looming prow;—
    Still hears the voices of that silent band;
He waits to join them in their grateful vow
    To Him, who sways the sea and rules the land:—
A mirage of the brain's unrestful sleep;—
A myth of echoes from the voiceless deep.

XIX.

His anxious gaze, fixed on the horizon's verge,
    Scanneth the line which boundeth sea and skies;
He listens mutely to the breaking surge,
    As on the sandy shore it faintly dies.
Soft are the notes of Ocean's funeral dirge,—
    As echoes which the murmuring sea-shell sighs;
And light as beauty, calm as heaven the wave,
Which shrouds the shipwrecked in their ocean grave.

XX.

White winged bird of Ocean, thou art gone!
    Lone wanderer over many a lonely sea;
No more thy gallant prow shall greet the dawn;
    All latitudes are now alike to thee;
Thy longitude is run! The waves have borne
    Thee home,—with thy broad pinions fluttering free!
Farewell: no storm shall touch thee with emotion;
Rest in the bosom of thine own loved Ocean.

XXI.

Thus pass the brave and beautiful away
   To that dim, silent, shadowy region, where
The sickly beams of labor-loving day
   Light no false hopes to vanish in despair.
Sweet solitude! There human agony
   Is hushed! Tranquillity reigns ever there!
Dark Hades! in thy quietude so blest,
Each weary mortal is a welcome guest.

XXII.

Around a rock's rude point, hard by the shore,
   Swift as an arrow from the elastic bow,
A light canoe, with palm leaves covered o'er,
   Moved beachward, softly as a flake of snow:
In haste, four maskers from the shallop bore,
   Wrapt in the dark habiliments of woe,
A seeming slumberer in their sturdy arms,
Whose form betrays a thousand hidden charms.

XXIII.

Her half-veiled neck with dimpling beauties fraught,
   A snow-wreath blooming with the warmth of blushes;
An ivory pillow tastefully inwrought
   With rose-tint pearl, shows that life's current gushes
In thread-like streams, as delicate as thought,
   When first love's fancy in confusion rushes
Over the young brow, radiant as morn,
And chaste as cloudlets floating in the dawn.

XXIV.

One raven-ringlet from her tresses straying,—
   A sisterhood enravishingly fair,
Adown her neck was innocently playing
   In charmful circles with the wanton air.
When Cupid fain would conquer by delaying,
   His labyrinthic castle is the hair,
Whence he lets fly full many a wounding dart,
Till he doth capture the rebellious heart.

XXV.

Anselmo, starting from his musing mood,
   Gazed with surprise on this mysterious scene:
Conflicting passions kindled in his blood;
   Dark shadows flitted thwart his brow serene;
Hope, fear, revenge, in a tumultuous flood,
   Burst from his heart as though they long had been
Imprisoned there: so mountain torrents flow,
When summer suns dissolve their hoarded snow.

XXVI.

He sees before him now his cherished bride;—
   The long-lost Idol of his mournful soul;
Now feels within his bosom gently glide,
   Like sunbeams when the morning mists uproll,
The gallant spirits of his youthful pride,
   Charming his passions to their fond control:
Love beams refulgent from his humid eyes;
Smiles light his brow; his heart dissolves in sighs.

XXVII.

While gazing thus, some spark of hallowed fire
  Touched her pale lips, relumed her languid eyes;
She bent on him one glance of soft desire;—
  His doubts dispel,—despair, defeated flies;
Love's gushing tides flow deeper, broader, higher,
  Full as the ocean, boundless as the skies:
His soul expandeth with the potent charm,
An Angel's power nerves his single arm.

XXVIII.

One effort sets the lovely prisoner free;
  He boldly bids the unknown tyrants draw;
From hidden scabbards, with celerity,
  Four shining blades leapt forth: unmoved he saw,
Nor did repent his own temerity;—
  Nor would he, had there been as many more:
He dreads no fiend, he fears no power above,
Whose heart throbs with the high impulse of love.

XXIX.

His foot he firmly planted on the ground,
  With the assurance faith and love impart:
His well aimed blow right through the corselet found
  Of the first masker, entrance to his heart;
Leaping in air with a convulsive bound,
  His craven spirit swiftly did depart
From its base consort, and with deep remorse,
Bequeathed to earth another mouldering corse:

XXX.

And as the lifeless trunk rolled on the shore,
   A broken mask presented to the sight,
The face of Bolus who long while before,
   At Juan's command, led Julia from the light
Of life and love,—did cruelly immure
   Her in dark cells of soul-corroding night:—
His base-born spirit, with the swift descent
Of ponderous guilt, to Tophet downward went.

XXXI.

Scorning at first advantage of the foe
   Who boldly bade them all at once, come on;
Now, when they saw him lay their comrade low,
   Their ire well nigh their courtesy had won:
Their second champion parried a fearful blow,—
   Then gave a thrust which well its work had done,
But that ANSELMO saw the aim he took,—
And seeing, bent aside, and shunned the stroke.

XXXII.

Now foot to foot the combat they renew;
   Their strokes less art than furiousness betray;
Shame that each steel did not its duty do,
   Kindleth in both resentment and dismay;—
Their blades were never wont to prove untrue,—
   Each fears a moment he may lose the day:
Full soon each brings his spirit in command,
And wields his weapon with a master's hand.

XXXIII.

The masker had the vantage of his foe,
    In that, unseen, he saw ANSELMO's face;
Skill, strength, revenge were stamped on every blow,
    As one who ancient memories would efface:
But when he saw his own blood freely flow,
    With rage he shook, grew furious with disgrace,
And madly strove by fierceness and by fraud,
In his brave foe to sheathe his murderous sword.

XXXIV.

As the wild boar by Carib lances wounded,
    Turns on his fell pursuers with defiance;
Foaming with rage, by wound on wound astounded,
    Bites the dull earth, with death seeks grim affiance,
So were the masker's blows,—his wrath unbounded,
    Despair destroyed the art of their appliance:
ANSELMO struck a direful stroke,—the head
And spirit of his foe together fled.

XXXV.

The gory head rolled on the sandy plain;
    The face, distorted with fierce passion, seemed
To darken with the agony of pain,
    And with the glare of bitter vengeance gleamed,—
A map combining every guilty stain
    Of which a base assassin ever dreamed:
In heart, coyote; in spirit, a hyena,
Down rushed Kaznoe to his own place—Gehenna.

XXXVI.

No longer the survivors would refrain
   From joint combat with their adversary,
Who, single-handed had their comrades slain,—
   Their courtesy no more their fear would carry:
His prowess they admire, still both disdain
   To yield unconquered; or, let conquest tarry,
Till one by one, his triumph they forestall,
Or like their comrades in the conflict fall.

XXXVII.

But ere they rush to blows, this parley, brief,
   Gave to ANSELMO a few moments rest:
Whence, comes thy phrenzy, stranger? Is it grief?
   Or sits despair enthroned within thy breast?
In carnage surely love finds no relief;
   Desist the unequal combat, and be blest:
Earth hath no surplus of the brave and good,
That thou shouldst recklessly thus shed thy blood.

XXXVIII.

To whom, ANSELMO: Senores, life to me,
   Dawned soft and beautiful as opening day;
My youth was a delightful reverie,
   Blending the subtle, unrefractive ray
Of lofty science with the imagery
   Of plastic fancy—fondly fair and gay;—
Rich and transparent as yon cloudlets seem
Floating in light, dissolving in a gleam.

XXXIX.

As zephyrs wafting through Losario's grove,
  Inhale the fragrance their light pinions shed,
When at the eventide they wanton rove,
  Amid yon Isles with fadeless bloom o'erspread,—
So, then I felt the balmy breath of love
  O'er all my passions, thoughts and feelings spread;
Pure as the halo of a morning dream,—
Voluptuous as Elysia's rosy stream.

XL.

Earth hath no scene so fair, mists may not mar;
  Earth's brightest hopes fade like the fallen leaf;
Dark clouds obscured my spirit's guiding star;
  I drank the gall and wormwood of grief:
I wandered many a moon—I wandered far,
  Nor change, nor time gave my sad heart relief:
The past, the future mingle in this hour,—
My love lies shrouded in yon bruised flower.

XLI.

Unworthy yonder Chief of swords so true:
  He won by stealth the gem he holds by force;
He dares dark deeds, he yet shall live to rue;
  Death's racking pangs were joy to his remorse;
And ye, who nerve his arm, alike imbue
  Your souls in guilt,—Is this your sole resource
For bread? Noble Senores! Aim well; strike sure;
Else soon ye wander on death's shadowy shore.

J

XLII.

Full soon the combat fiercely is renewed;
   Their swords out-gleam the sun's unclouded light;
The clashing steel, impurplingly imbrued,
   Startles the slumbering air with pale affright;
Love's hero never yet hath been subdued;
   Love arms her champions with resistless might;
Alike fair Helen and immortal Jove,
Proclaim thy majesty all-conquering love!

XLIII.

Anselmo watcheth well his wary foes;
   With skill and grace he guides his good right hand;
Each thrust, each parry to them plainly shows,
   A master's art directs his dripping brand,
Anon, he wardeth off their double blows;—
   Now strikes,—and now retires upon the strand;—
Then fiercely makes on them a furious charge,
Which both their anger and their wounds enlarge.

XLIV.

Back to the boat the Bishop bore his prize,
   And left her there in charge of trusty slaves,—
For in this strange and soldier-like disguise,
   Was the young Bishop Juan:—so lust depraves
The noblest of our race: his glistening eyes,
   Like sunbeams glowing on the glittering waves,
Gloat like an amateur's on the strife,
Disporting fatally with human life.

XLV.

He gazed upon the conflict with delight;
    His presence with more zeal his friends inspire;
Anselmo grew heroic in his sight,—
    His art sublime—his execution dire:
Nor till the third fell in the fearful fight,—
    Nor till the fourth was ready to expire,
Did Juan draw forth his burnished blade to quell,
This stranger champion of fair Isabel.

XLVI.

Now face to face the rivals proudly stand;
    Each greets the other's gaze with withering smile;
Anon, their blows ring out from hand to hand;
    Each strives by art the other to beguile:
Now forward bent—now kneeling on the sand;
    Impurpling dews their glittering steels defile;
Then back a pace each from his foe retires;
While each the other's skill and strength admires.

XLVII.

Respite renewed their strength and their offense;
    Long while they fought—weary and faint they fought;
Alike in the attack and the defense,
    Less force than art is to the contest brought:
Meanwhile fair victory fluttered in suspense,
    Doubted by both—by both devoutly sought;
While thus the exhausting combat they sustain,
A cavalier comes sweeping o'er the plain:

XLVIII.

Onward he comes—by all but one unseen—
    The trusty slave who keepeth watch and ward,
He knew the horsemen by his gallant mien,—
    His light-foot steed scarce touching the green sward;
His white sombrero with its plume of green—
    His red serapo flowing all abroad:
He knew it was his master's bitterest foe,
The bold and daring mountain chief,—Pedro.

XLIX.

And though he knew the Bishop would delight
    In single combat with this far-famed chief;
He wisely judged that in his present plight,
    He had less need of foes than of relief:
With wary step,—while tottering in the fight,
    Suiting the action to his message brief,
He cried, beware! and round his master threw
His arms, and bore him off to the canoe.

L.

Scarce had he pushed the shallop from the shore,
    When Don Pedro dashed in the foaming wave;
His sabre circling high in air,—he swore,
    The surf should be the priestly-soldier's grave:
The oath was lost in air,—a moment more,
    The surge receding bore the Bishop, brave,
Beyond the reach of his fierce adversary:
The shallop was his fort and sanctuary.

LI.

And little did he reck for many days
    And many weary nights his dangerous state;
Nor did his lips accuse, nor did they praise
    The good, or evil of his passing state:
Alike, amidst the glow of fever's rays,
    And the dense mist of passion and of hate,
He calmly waited the returning hour,
Of wonted healthfulness and conscious power.

LII.

Meanwhile, ANSELMO, weary, bleeding, faint,
    Sank on one knee upon the sanguine sand;
Leaned on his sword, as calmly as a saint,
    Awaits his summons to the heavenly land.
He did not move, nor did he make complaint;
    He was too faint to speak, too weak to stand:
He made a virtue of necessity,
And kept the field—a proud felicity.

LIII.

And long as victor would have kept the field;
    Have sealed his triumph with his latest breath;
Have crowned the conquest which he would not yield,
    By grim alliance with resistless death:
Have left earth's wrongful judgment unrepealed;
    His name and honor things of fleeting breath;
But that Don Pedro kindly took him thence,
To his own mountain refuge and defense.

LIV.

Far up the craggy steeps, where foot of man
    Seldom hath prest the light and crumbling soil,
On a rude, rustic willow-wreathed sedan,
    With careful step and hours of weary toil,
Two faithful veterans of Don Pedro's clan,
    Unurged by bribes, or hope of victor's spoil,
Bore their unconscious burden to a grove,
Where peace and joy might ever dwell with love.

LV.

The reverend palms lift up their heads on high,
    With the calm bliss of conscious inspiration;
Their boughs umbrageous breathe a gentle sigh,
    As they behold, with chastened admiration,
Their deep green shadows mingling with the sky,
    Its lights and shades in beauteous variation;
A living picture set in softened glow,
Reflected from the placid lake below.

XVI.

The grass crept softly down the flowery glade,
    To deck its margin with a fringe of green;
The graceful lily sweet obeisance made,
    Laving her fair cheek in the liquid sheen:
The rose, a tribute of affection paid,
    With vestal beauty, blooming and serene,
Bent from her wild-briar down, as from a throne,
And kissed the Lake with passion Love might own.

LVII.

Even the rocks were dutiful: they seemed
   To greet the sportive wavelets with delight,
Clad in moss velvet wherein violets beamed,
   Like stars in the soft azure depths of night,
Their grave and meditative features gleamed
   With softer radiance in her liquid light:
A sacred grotto like a sanctuary,
Forming a solitude not solitary.

LVII.

A solitude made vocal with the lays
   Of birds, of fairest hue and richest tone,
Where tuneful echo on her lyre plays
   Their various notes as if they were her own;
Where silence murmurs with melodious praise,
   And lonely pensiveness is not alone:
A quietude where loving spirits throng,
The hours of peaceful pleasure to prolong.

LIX.

This was the sanctuary of a sage,
   Who humbly sought communion with the blest:
No earthly balm can bitter grief assuage;
   No cordial lull the troubled soul to rest;
His flowing locks were silvered o'er with age,
   His beard in ample folds fell on his breast;
His brow was calm, his large dark eye serene,
His form erect and dignified his mien.

LX.

Devotion wafted all his thoughts on high!
   At morn, communing with the holy spirit,
Entranced, he saw, with faith-illumined eye,
   The glorious mansions, which the saints inherit:
Unchallenged passed the portals of the sky,
   And walked the empyrean like a spirit;
Resting at eve, where light immortal shone,
He, with the Elders, bowed before the throne.

LXI.

There was a partner of his solitude;
   The only tie which bound his soul to earth;
The image of her whom he early wooed,
   Whose life was forfeit to her first-born's birth;
A daughter blooming into womanhood,
   Her beauty the fair index of her worth;
Fair as a blossom on a crystal stream;—
No care had yet disturbed her young life's dream,

LXII.

And oh, how beautiful! Her golden hair,
   Waving in sunlight paled its richest beams;
Than driven snow, her marble brow more fair,
   Her soft blue eyes with love's pure starlight gleams;
Her smile with beauty lights the ambient air;—
   Lovely, as those who visit us in dreams;
The warm blush on her cheek more rich than wine,
More delicate than lilies, pure, divine.

LXIII.

Leila was happy in her mountain home!
  Her chief delight, her cherished filial love;
She had no wish in the gay world to roam;
  She knew each bird and flower in all the grove;
And when she gazed up in the starry dome,
  Saw sister-angels smiling from above:
Heard the seraphic songs which grace inspire;—
And sighing, yearned to join the heavenly choir.

LXIV.

Happy as beautiful! She did not dream
  A true, pure heart could glow with passion's flame;
A crystal fount send forth a turbid stream;
  A holy sympathy awaken shame;
That the bright sun had shone with lurid gleam;
  That from shekina clouds of darkness came:—
That on the altar of the heart in turn,
All hopes may kindle and all passions burn.

LXV.

When first she saw ANSELMO, weary, faint;
  Alike unconscious of his friends and fate;
Sweet pity freed her bosom from restraint;
  She joined her sire to soothe his hapless state:
Full many an anxious hour, without complaint,
  Alone, o'er the scarce breathing youth, she sate,
Watching the sufferer with more tender care,
His life became the burthen of her prayer!

LXVI.

The unvibrating beam of poising time,
  Long while 'twixt life and death its balance held;
No struggling groan with inharmonious chime,
  Fell from Anselmo's lips; no eye beheld
A gesture of impatience; calm, sublime,
  The union pain with quietude did weld:
His life hung trembling on a broken breath,
As o'er a fount a vapor quivereth!

LXVII.

Twas morn: upon his cold and pallid face,
  A tremulous gleam of golden sunlight fell;
In its chaste glow, the eye of love did trace
  An Angel breaking death's mysterious spell:
Her prayers attest her trust in heavenly grace,—
  Tumultuous passions in her bosom swell:
In gratitude for health's returning bliss,
Fair Leila on his brow imprest a kiss.

LXVIII.

The kiss of love, the fount of health unsealeth;
  Anselmo owned its touch of quickening power;
A warm flush o'er his features softly stealeth;—
  Each moment seemeth like a lingering hour;
Is it an Angel's form the light revealeth,
  Now bending o'er him like a drooping flower?
Over her young heart's firmament—her face—
Love's blushing borealis he doth trace.

LIX.

A flush was on her cheeks: her thoughts withdrew
  From lake, and trees, and flowers: alas, she felt,
That in the Eden of her spirit grew
  A passion, to which all her passions knelt!
May not one cherished thought the soul imbue?
  One vivid spark the purest diamond melt?
She felt her breast dissolving in a flame,
Yet knew not what it was, or whence it came.

LXX.

How brief the hours,—how rapid in their flight—
  When borne on rosy love's expanding wing?
We scarcely sip the nectar of delight,
  Ere we anticipate the serpent's sting:
Fast fades the bloom of beauty in dim night,—
  And keenest pangs from richest pleasures spring:
So sitting by the grave ANSELMO's side,
The pensive Leila mused at even-tide

LXXI.

Too sad for thee this tranquil sunset scene!
  ANSELMO, go; we must not linger here:
Dark shadows of the future flit between
  Us! Dost thou not see them? Hist thee! Nor hear
Their mimic chatterings in yon ivy-green?
  Their tiny wings beat on the ambient air!
Ah, me, the fancies which our childhood trace,
No lore illumes; no time can e'er efface.

LXXII.

Hearest thou not, ANSELMO? Go away;
    The evening shadows soon will gather round:
Thou dost enjoy the smile of opening day,
    More than the richest sunsets ever found:
Morn rouses man from sleep's dull roundelay,
    To fight life's battle till death's trump shall sound:
The gorgeous clouds of yonder burnished West,
To my lorn heart are Day's funereal vest.

LXXIII.

Go, dear ANSELMO; leave me here, forlorn:
    The pensive beauty of this hour doth wake
Sweet thoughts of immortality! Thus upborne,
    I love,—yet live! Can love our being take?
Has thou not said, at eve and rosy morn,
    As oft we lingered by this placid lake,
That like this mountain daughter of the Ocean,
Pure hearts responsive throb with love's emotion?

LXXIV.

Thou art not free to love: still thou art free:
    Go! Pray that my reverenced sire meet me here:
The world awaits thee: oh, I fain would be
    Thy slave! vain wish,—alas, this gushing tear
Attests my weakness! Thou canst'not love me!
    My frail fond heart, say, wherefore dost thou fear?
Go! And when morn salutes thy loving eyes,
My soul shall be as tranquil as the skies.

LXXV.

Is that an angel band I see descending?
  My home immortal is on yon bright shore!
Like yonder clouds with brighter hues ascending,
  Oh, let my lingering thoughts divinely soar!
And like yon brilliant bow of promise bending,
  Oh, let me bow to Him I should adore!
Adios, Laguna—flowers—birds and grove;
Your Leila fainteth with excess of love.

LXXVI.

Kneeling! Alone! She lifts her eyes to heaven;
  Her lily hands are folded on her breast;
Her face gleams with the various hues of even,
  Sublime in its emotions and its rest;
As if some youthful angel's kiss had given
  It all the finest features of the blest:
Her rose-bud lips, like opening flowers above,
Dispart with softest harmonies of love.

LXXVII.

Through all the grove deep silence reigned awhile—
  Deep as when death's dark angel lingereth nigh:
Her gentle heart had broken! Still the smile
  Of love was on her lips! So calm her eye,
Beauty in slumber could not more beguile!
  Her spirit wafted heavenward on a sigh!
The sage restrains his tears—the father groans—
The silence breaks—the grove responsive moans.

ANSELMO.

CANTO FIFTH.

I.

Beneath the branches of a princely palm,
   Anselmo sought the shadow of a rock,
Whose time-worn summit, midst all changes calm,
   Gave shelter to the shepherd and his flock;
From whose chaste granite breasts a liquid balm,
   Like dew-drops, oozed softly down to mock,
With humid air and gentle pattering,
The murmuring music of a bubbling spring.

II.

Prone on the springing streamlet's velveting
   Of yielding grasses and convolving flowers,
With many mingling vernal sweets, exhaling
   A perfume potent with dissolving powers,
He listened to the plaintive caroling
   Of beauteous birds, until the morning hours
Had passed the glowing point of culmination,
When noon-tide pants for evening recreation.

III.

Here slumber in the halo of a dream,
  Relumed soft memories with a holier light;
Once more he lingered by the silvery stream
  With her whose smile made all his boyhood bright.
He sighed—"Oh, that I were the sage I seem;
  Cold—calm and confident when in the sight
Of the world's busy multitude, who feel
That gold doth temper human hearts with steel

IV.

There is a tone—a silvery tone of love,
  Whose charmful intonations on the heart
Of youth, vibrates accordant as above,
  Angelic numbers harmonies dispart;
And though long years through varied climes he roves,
  Its warbling echoes evermore impart
Those symphonies in which true hearts rejoice—
It is the melody of girlhood's voice.

V.

There is a tone so full, so rich, so deep,
  So fraught with all that music can inspire,
That its soft cadence makes the miser weep;
  Kindleth in frost-bound hearts poetic fire;
Lulleth the maniac to dreamful sleep;
  Lureth young seraphs from the heavenly choir,
To tune their golden harps at her fair shrine—
'Tis woman's voice enriched by love divine.

VI.

There is a beauty in the vestal rose,
    Gracing the forest, on its sweet wild-brier;
So chastely delicate in its repose,
    Man gazeth on it only to admire;
Delicious fragrance from its petals flows,
    Inspiring bliss, repressing warm desire—
So beautiful and with such virgin grace,
Sweet girlhood charms the boldest of our race.

VII.

There is a beauty in the full-blown rose,
    Reigning resplendent as the queen of flowers;
Each beauteous leaf with warmer blushes glows,
    And richer perfumes fill her fragrant bowers;
Graceful in port, voluptuous in repose,
    None may dispute her right to regal powers:
So beautiful, so rightful the proud sway
Of lovely woman in maturity.

VIII.

Beauty sequestered in the flowery vale,
    Is strong in her serene obscurity;
Shielded by mountains from the ruder gale,
    Bloometh sweetly-sportive to maturity;
Shakes every reef from out love's silken sail,
    Glides down life's stream in fond security;
Nor heeds the change of wind, nor turn of tide,
One loving pilot is her only guide.

IX.

Beauty transplanted to the sunnier clime,
    Where fashion smiles on virtue with disdain,
Bloometh richly and more beautiful as Time
    Unrols the titles of her right to reign:
Her holy glance rebuketh hoary crime;
    Lechers adore the love they dare not stain;
Her smile, like sun-beams, all pollution spurns;
Her love grows purer as it brighter burns.

X.

So sweet the tones now falling on his ear;
    Rich as the mellow music of the morn;
So beautiful to him doth she appear,
    Who was so rudely from his presence torn;
Hath she indeed escaped the fowler's snare,
    With all her vestal loveliness unshorn?
May not real joys be so divine, they seem
The airy pleasures of a golden dream?

XI.

Sweet memories came with love-enshrined beams,
    Lightly as stars patrol the realms of night,
Shedding soft lustre on those distant streams,
    Where first in solitude he sought delight;
Where, rapt with ecstacies of young love's dreams,
    His soul entranced beheld that child of light,
Whose spirit as an angel guard was given,
To cheer his heart and guide his steps to heaven.

XII.

He murmured, IsABEL! His pallid face
    Flushed with the softening gleams of fond emotion;
His kindling brow consumed the latent trace
    Of care, and glistened with sublime devotion;
His burning lips dissolved in liquid grace,
    Flowing from mellow rose-lips in commotion,
His arms with fancied pressure were entwining
The lovely being on his breast reclining.

XIII.

A maiden o'er a crystal fountain blushing,
    Enamoured of her own reflected charms;
A youth enraptured with the impetuous rushing
    Of passion's torrent in its first alarms;
A lover struggling in the grateful gushing
    Of love's spring-tide, and young love's rosy arms,
Enjoy a banquet of exquisite pleasure—
A bounded bliss, which hath a certain measure:

XIV.

Boundless the bliss, priceless the richer treasure,
    Excelling far in measure and degree,
The heighth and depth of that immortal pleasure
    Which love, when chastened with adversity,
Pours in the heart with unrestricted measure,
    As rivers pour their fulness in the sea;
True hearts dissolve, commingle and refine;
And kindred souls breathe fellowship divine.

XV.

Subdued by transports, enervate of bliss,
  Anselmo yieldeth to his phantom prize;
In fancy sips the nectar of her kiss;
  Still hears the mellow murmuring of her sighs;
Dreams not of joys in other worlds like this;
  Drinks deep salvation from her loving eyes;
"We part to meet again"—was gently spoken,
"The orange blossom is our mutual token."

XVI.

Who would not dare the dreary shades below,
  The sublimated joys of angels shun,
To prove the softer, richer, deeper glow
  Of woman's love, in loving raptures won?
One hour of love amends an age of woe;
  One gleam of love outshines the eternal sun:
He liveth not in vain to whom is given
Love's hour, which balanceth the bliss of heaven.

XVII..

From the warm embrace of the fiery sun,
  Exhausted Day adown the glowing west,
With light opprest, sank languidly upon
  Its gorgeous couch of clouds, as on the breast,
Of mothers, infants sink—till one by one
  The stars shone out on the cerulean vest,
In which from olden time, majestic night,
Arrays herself to give the world delight.

XVIII.

From her gem-azure drapery, replete
   With balmy odors and enchanting dreams,
Fell mist-like, soporiferously sweet,
   O'er the departing Day her chastening gleams;
Her breath of fragrance for young seraphs meet,
   Mingled with the melody of purling streams,
Whose velvet banks embossed with fadeless flowers,
Beguile love-laden youth from weary hours.

XIX.

In vain the beautifully pensive Eve
   Bent o'er the fainting Day—for he expired:
She mourned the ills her skill could not relieve,
   Yielded the prize to which her hope aspired;
Buoyant, her starry pinions poised, to leave
   The saddening scene, when with new thoughts inspired,
By the mellifluous charms of love and mirth,
She lingered to behold the joys of earth.

XX.

Airy and spacious were the lofty halls,
   Resembling more a suit of sylvan bowers;
The tapestry which gracèd the springing walls,
   Was jasmine woven with Biura flowers,
Forming a canopy for water-falls
   Descending in soft aromatic showers;
No net-work barred the perfumed breath of even,
No dome shut out the starry vault of heaven.

XXI.

And there were avenues of fragrant lime,
    O'er-arching smooth, broad tessalated aisles,
Strewn with the blossoms of a tropic clime;
    The intersections—Palo de buba Isles,
Floating in crystal founts; like those where Time
    Soothes grief with love, crowns age with dimpling
Ambrosial islands of a far off sea,   [smiles;
Where beauty blooms in immortality.

XXII.

The air effulgent suffused mellow light.
    Above, below through dales and fragrant groves;
So soft and rich, so roseate and bright,
    Tinting the visual orbs like those of doves,
Languor's voluptuous pressure on the sight,
    The luminous aroma of young loves;
Mysterious radiance of commingling beams;
Where shades are real—realities are dreams.

XXIII.

Around the fountains laughing boys were playing,
    And timid girls a sweet approval smiling;
Lovers beneath the clustering vines were straying;
    Each other with fond blandishments beguiling;
Lovers of pleasure in cool grottoes—staying   [whiling
    Their tastes with fruit and wine; each class thus
Away the prelude of the festival,
Which crowns with glory the high carnival.

XXIV.

Diffusive bliss, like lentulus and thyme,
  In dreamfulness each drowsy sense was sealing,
When, like deep thunder from a far-off clime,
  Music rent the air—her loudest tones were pealing;—
Then softened to a distance—mellowing chime, [ing:
  Like vernal zephyrs through young palm groves steal⁻
The lark sprang up on high to hail the dawn,
And chanticleer proclaimed the opening morn.

XXV.

Young life exultant from love's drowsy dreams,
  Bounded with lightsome step and tuneful measure;
And from the grottoes' cool refreshing streams,
  Came forth in bands, the elder heirs of pleasure;
All faces joyful with harmonious gleams
  Of love's first, latest, renovated treasure:
A gay, glad, gleeful, gratulatory throng,
Blending together in the dance and song.

XXVI.

A world in miniature; a strain transposes
  Each jocund dancer to the other's place;
Another strain—the vista half-discloses,
  Measuring the figure with excelling grace,
Erato, crowned with myrtles and with roses,
  Leading the dance—a fairy troupe who trace
The mazy labyrinths of the winding measure,
Whose chaste variety gives constant pleasure.

XXVII.

Growing more merry with increasing mirth,
    Alike forgetful of disparity;
None urge the claims of place—the pride of birth:
    Wealth waltzeth on with matron charity;
Legates of heaven dance minuets of earth;
    Proud learning polkas with hilarity:
Music creative as the blast Abanga,
Mingles all measures in the grave Fandango.

XVIII.

Evening still lingered in the western sky,
    Charmed with the harmless gayeties of mortals;
The moon, from her light fleecy throne on high,
    Shed softest radiance through the leafy portals,
Blending her charms with zephyr's warmer sigh,
    Which, lovers breathing, soon become immortals,
Bidding adieu to earthly cares and blisses,
They feast on smiles, luxuriate in kisses.

XXIX.

And night came on—the deep and solemn night,
    The beautiful, the grand and the sublime,
Arrayed in brilliant robes of changeless light,
    Paused in her proud and lofty march with Time;
Gazing a moment on the lovely sight,
    So perfect in its beauty and its chime;
A tear-drop glistened in her gracious eye,
Prophetic of some scene of sorrow nigh.

XXX.

And merry maskers came; a motley band
    Of youth, of wit, of beauty and of grace;
Here one with inert age twirls hand in hand,
    Another peereth in some younger face;
Like meteors bursting o'er a luminos strand;
    Like comets streaming through star-radiant space:
All praise the splendor of the coruscation;
All hail with joy the blissful inspiration.

XXXI.

A monologue, in foreign accent, charms;
    A dulcet voice trills forth a monody;
A duet, tremulous with love's alarms,
    Discourse soul-captivating melody;
Triplets in tritones, gravity disarms;
    And quartets warble softest symphony:
Anon, all in harmonious chorus join,
Heavenly the strain, the fellowship divine.

XXXII.

And there was One, whose princely gait inspired
    In all a more than wonted deference;
Whose graceful measure all the fair admired,
    And sought his hand with anxious preference;
Who sought him seemed by him to be desired;
    In courteous phrase and without reference
To age, to wit, to beauty or to station,
He charmed the moments of each gay flirtation.

XXXIII.

His rich, deep, voice rang out in tones so clear,
   So fraught with patient hope and burning love,
The fragrant groves and softly luminous air,
   Seemed vocal with strains floating from above,—
Triumphant rhapsodies of conquering prayer,—
   Warblings more plaintive than the pensive dove:
A Roman toga, his disguise, pro tanto;
His symbol the fair Espirito Santo.

XXXIV.

In his right hand, by wreathlets well disguised,
   He held a rose geranium with care,
A gift of love, by him too highly prized,
   To proffer undistinguished to the fair;
Designed for her whose beauty realized
   The loveable ideal—light as air,
And luminous as light; the fond heart's goal,
The magellanic cloudlet of the soul.

XXXV.

Hail, love's effulgence! An admiring tone,
   Greets beauty waltzing the emblossomed aisle;
Graceful as Valisneria floats the Rhone;
   Or, zephyr-wafting Visca soars the Nile;
Blooming as Venus on night's brow alone,
   Charming as rosy dawn's awakening smile:
Sweet voices murmur rapturous admiration,
A shout proclaims the general approbation.

XXXVI.

Softly as Spring's infantile dew-drop presses
   On fair Mimosa's chastely-yielding breast;
Gently as starlight streameth, like love's tresses,
   Adown the glowing mountains of the West;
Lightly as vernal loves, in summer dresses,
   Come in our dreams with rapturous unrest;
So did her lightsome measure o'er the blossoms
Stir the fond memories of faithful bosoms.

XXXVII.

Her gauze-like trail, the smooth mosaic sweeping,
   Graceful as fleecy cloudlets thwart the sky;
Then rising in light folds, as chastely sleeping
   On her voluptuous form, as though no eye
Beheld the dimpling charms beneath them peeping,
   Moved by the slight emotions of a sigh:
Like violets from their mossy dells emerging;
Like wavelets over blushing coral surging.

XXXVIII.

White roses on her blushing temples prest,
   Soft love-knots of a dewey myrtle wreath,
Whence o'er her ivory neck and snowy breast,
   To shade from vulgar gaze the charms beneath,
A roseate veil fell like a fluttering vest,
   Light as the mist on mirrors maidens breathe;
Rich as the shadowy masquerade of even,
It gave the charms it hid the hues of heaven.

XXXIX.

On her fair smoothen brow, less to illume
    Than absorb purer rays, a diamond shone;
White as the driven snow, a downy plume
    Bent o'er her shining braids—an ebon throne,
Where like a queen, luxuriant of bloom,
    A budding moss-rose calmly reigned alone;
A symbol of that sweet angelic merit,
Which virtue robed in beauty doth inherit.

XL.

Soft as the music of the winding stream
    To weary pilgrims in a desert place;
Sweet as the murmurs of her first-born's dream
    To the young mother gazing on his face;
Rapt as the rise and fall, to lovers seem,
    Of passion's tide, infused with love and grace—
So rose and fell the oft repeated strain,
Hail! Thou the loveliest of beauty's train.

XLI.

Pleasure dipt her pencil in the fount of love,
    And with soft touches did each face relume;
More fond emotions gentler bosoms move,
    Star-glances soften, shadowy brows illume;
Over the vermeil cheek love's dimples rove
    Mid smiles suffusing more angelic bloom—
Beauty foldeth pleasure in her rosy arms,
And sportive pleasure crowneth beauty's charms.

XLII.

In the fine texture of the human heart, [sure,
   Which throbs the depth of woe, the heighth of plea-
There is inwoven in its holiest part
   A thread of first-love, which sustains the pressure,
Of all the crushing ills neglect and art
   Inflict in bitter draught and boundless measure;
Which, when all other heart-woof fades, decays,
Holds young-life's warp in love of other days.

XLIII.

Hath that fine harp of universal tone,
   Which mortals sweep with unsurpassing art;
Whose music charms the monarch on his throne,
   And equal bliss to peasants doth impart,
Alike in torrid clime and frozen zone,
   Nature's melodeon—a mother's heart—
A chord which doth midst every change rejoice
In tones responsive to her offspring's voice?

XLIV.

Harp of mysterious power, thou lover's heart!
   Lyre of priceless worth and countless treasure!
Thy sounding numbers spurn the touch of Art;
   Sighs sweep vibrations of tumultuous pleasure;
Thy thoughts of fire rapt melodies impart;
   Love's line of beauty is thy boundless measure:
Bards bend extatic o'er thy tuneful slumbers;
Gods hear delirious thine immortal numbers!

XLV.

A glance may fascinate a noble soul;
   A piercing gaze unbend the lion's crest;
A deep, dark, daring, dazzling eye control
   The stormy passions of the human breast;
The azure eye of love, from pole to pole,
   Disturb, and give the troubled spirit rest:
But all the varying language of the eye
Hath not the pathos of a murmuring sigh.

XLVI.

Her sigh of love awakes the slumbering lyre;
   Her breath of music stirs its tuneful dreams;
Her thoughts responsive melodies inspire,
   Till warbling echoes, like commingling streams,
Flow in voluptuous measure! Soft desire
   And love illume all eyes with fondest gleams:
In dreamy, rapturous silence all rejoice—
   Charmed with the mellow music of her voice:

1.

How sweet the first transports of joy which endeareth!
   How blissful the thought of hearts mingled in one;
When love in the shadowy distance appeareth,
   As through showers appeareth the radiant sun;
And every moment, by anticipation,
We drink deeper draughts, though with insatiation
Of fountains o'erflowing with gratification,
   And desire and bliss, in the bower of love.

2.

Oh, sweeter by far, when the fond heart enjoyeth,
    The fullness of pleasure which one-ness imparts;
Each draught more delicious and deeper, nor cloyeth
    The gush of delight from sweet union of hearts!
And broader and richer the stream from each flowing;
The flame of affection more ardently glowing,
We mingle together, like fountains o'erflowing,
    And dove-like inhabit the bower of love!

3.

Oh, sweetest of all, when the sad heart reposes
    Serenely and soft on the bosom of love;
When thornless the pillow, though fading the roses,
    Yet fragrant as flowerets blooming above!
We live o'er again in our fond recollection,
Those transports of joy sanctified by affection, [tion,
Which sunshine and showers have brought to perfec-
    In hallowed groves of the bower of love!

4.

ANSELMO, I come! Thou loved one of my childhood;
    Receive to thy bosom thy wandering dove!
The far off Potomac, its rocks and its wild-wood,
    Proclaim evermore our first sorrow and love!
Though care shadeth thy brow, those shadows are fairer
Than the bloom of young love! Than gems richer and
Love groweth not old; it grows gentler and dearer [rarer!
    Let thy bosom then be my own bower of love!

XLVII.

As rose-buds open to the gentle shower,
  So sweetly verse disparts her lips of pleasure;
Entranced, as young love's first enrapturing hour,
  The ambient air resounds the charmful measure!
The nightingale soars from her echoing bower, [ure!
  To hymn the strain—but droops with tuneful press.
Fraught with fine harmonies clouds soar above,
  And wondering seraphs sing the Bower of Love.

XLVIII.

Young Cupid, who beneath her jetty curls
  In ambush lay, began to burn and shiver;
His feverish brow with sweet delirium whirls—
  His hands grow cold—down fell his bow and quiver;
Grasping the glances of her eyes, he hurls
  Those shafts divine from love's own azure river,
Promiscuously midst that adoring throng—
A wild approval of the enchanting song.

XLIX.

Anselmo wondered at this new creation;
  His throbbing temples intense feeling flushing;
His heart responsive with strange palpitation,
  To the warm tides from out its caverns gushing—
Like mountain torrents over vegetation,
  Sweeping resistlessly—deepening—rushing;
He sprang to clasp this loveliest Israfel,
Raptly exclaiming, Hail! my Isabel!

L.

He of the princely gait had rushed before him;
    Had dared the flood which swept his soul away;
His love-delirium might well assure him
    That such wild phrenzy would his heart betray:
"I burn like the adoring seraphim,"
    Burst from his writhing lips in agony:
Charming in madness—in subduement grand,
He crushed the rose-geranium in his hand—

LI.

And flung the bruised odoriferous leaves,
    As though he had her chosen lover been!
Strong is the unseen network Passion weaves;
    Princes are spell-bound by her dazzling sheen;
She spares no victims, granteth no reprieves;
    Smiles on the tortures of her slaves serene;
Wrecks the adventurer whom her fires beguile,
And with the fragments rears his funeral pile.

LII.

ANSELMO's senses in rapt transports reeling,
    Felt not the wounding shock of rude collision;
Saw not the sinuous step of danger stealing
    Position whence to strike with dread precision;
One only sentiment absorbed all feeling,—
    One only object did engross his vision,—
A lily-hand with a rich orange blossom,
Resting full soothely on his fluttering bosom.

LIII.

Fierce as the ravening tiger tracks his prey;
  Swift as the bright bolt bursteth from the sky;
The masker flung his dark disguise away,
  And stood erect, and cried, "bold rival, die;"
A giant's arm were powerless to stay
  The poniard swift descending from on high,
By all, save love's keen glance, unseen:—where fell
The thirsty blade, there lay fair ISABEL.

LIV.

The rose-tint fadeth from her angel face;
  Impurpling streams distain her snowy vest;
Lifting her drooping eyes, she said, with grace,
  "Since thou art safe, my love, I sweetly rest!"
Death with dark lineaments refused to trace
  The lily resting on ANSELMO's breast:
While yet her shrinking life-pulse quivereth
His burning lips absorb her fleeting breath.

LV.

Back on his heart the Bishop felt the gush
  Of love, grief, guilt, a dark, remorseless flood;
His pallid temples were no longer flush
  With raging passion burning in his blood:
Despair o'erwhelmed him in her demon rush;
  Horror froze him to the spot whereon he stood;
Mute terror sealed his lips, convulsed his frame,
Rent his proud spirit, crushed his soul in shame.

LVI.

We mourn to see the blush of beauty fading
  Untimely from the downy cheek of youth;
To see the kind and virtuous retrograding
  From the blest paths of innocence and ruth;
To see the darksome cloud of falsehood shading
  The noble brow once luminous with truth:
We shrink to see the strong man bear alone
The stroke which hurls his reason from its throne.

LVII.

Doom me to grasp the lightning's fiery wing;
  To rush repellant midst storm-riven skies;
To wage war with Apollyon, and bring
  His demons forth as the sole-victor prize;
To brave with curses the Eternal King—
  With reason to direct the grand emprize:
These might I dare! But save me from the blight
Of reason wandering midst unbroken night.

LVIII.

There stood the Bishop Juan! Tall and erect;
  So late a noble specimen of man;
The prayerful Patriarch of God's elect;
  The boldest foe of Pedro's mountain clan;
His large blue eyes were glazed with retrospect,—
  To one sole point his thoughts converging ran:
His soul surcharging with the flood so fell,—
Burst in one shriek: "Alas, dear Isabel!"

LIX.

Beside him, hand in hand, Don Manuel
    And the fair Nun, sweet types of love and joy,
Lovely and beautiful, as poets tell,
    Were Cytherea and her darling Boy,—
Stood mutely gazing on the mystic spell,
    Which bound in chains, and threatened to destroy
Him, whom they sought, to challenge as a foe;
Him whom they found to pity for his woe.

LX.

And he beheld them! Did the charm beguile
    The fate which paralyzed his mighty soul?
A gushing tear-drop solved the film awhile;
    Back from his brow dark shadows slowly roll,—
His rigid face relaxeth to a smile,
    And reason momently resumes control:
On Manuel's head he laid his hand with joy,—
And calmly said—May Heaven bless thee, Boy!

LXI.

And she was there—the mother of that boy;
    And to his father's blessing response gave:
Pale Julia's heart was overwhelmed with joy,—
    Her voice to Juan a message from the grave!
Words fraught with sweet salvation may destroy!
    From destiny no mortal power can save:
Juan's fingers beat an idiotic patter;
His lips convulsive ran with senseless chatter.

LXII.

In boundless mercy pitying Heaven sent
   Her erring son a blessing in disguise;
A deafening shout the awful silence rent,—
   Pedro, the robber, stood before their eyes:
On his advancing foe the Bishop bent
   One maniac gaze—and swift as lightning flies,—
Rushed on him with demoniac might and main,—
Both bleeding, fell; and falling, both were slain.

LXIII.

The hours flung wide the portals of the Day;
   Night from her starry throne did gently glide;
The cannon echoing from the mole and bay,
   Proclaimed Don Carlos and his youthful bride:
The dreamless combatants were borne away;
   And left to sleep forever side by side!
The noble warrior, satiate with slaughter,
Embraced Don Manuel—and forgave his daughter!

LXIV.

Though over ISABEL all deeply mourned,
   Than in full life, she seemed more passing fair;
Divine repose her pallid brow adorned,
   Her sad face wore a sweet angelic air;
Even death was by her loveliness suborned,
   His dart uplifted—poised—he did not dare
To strike,—for, oh, so beautiful—so still—
Those silent charms did enervate his will.

LXV.

Droop not, my love, Anselmo lowly sighed;
    Droop not—thy head is pillowed on my breast;
Arrest the ebbing of Life's purple tide,
    And make this heart the haven of thy rest;
My beautiful! My spirit's cherished bride,
    Live! And my life shall be supremely blest:
Thou shalt not die! My breath shall be thy breath!
My kiss shall charm thee from the spell of Death!

LXVI.

Oh, Death! I know thou wilt be lenient, Death:
    'Tis but thy shadow which hath fallen here:
Nor life, nor love, nor beauty slumbereth
    More lovely! Death, thou hast no melting tear!
These gushing tears are the ethereal breath
    Of ministering Angels hovering near!
Oh, linger not, lest thy dread presence fright
Her gentle spirit from these realms of light.

LXVII.

The morning beams were on her tresses playing;
    Her pallid lips with prayer were gently riven;
O'er her calm brow some tender thoughts were straying
    Of life and love,—like shadows of the even;
The lights and shades evanishing, delaying,
    Were mingled tints of earth and hues of heaven:
A struggling sigh escaped her swelling bosom,
Tinging her cheeks with Life's reviving blossom.

XLVII.

She lives! She lives! ANSELMO raptly cried:
  The night hath passed, the daylight doth appear;
The storm hath swept the murky air aside,
  And winter's frost dissolves in Spring's warm tear!
Sweet Spring! Thou bringest to my long-sought bride,
  The buds and blossoms of love's opening year!
Immortal fruits and amaranthine flowers,
Shall crown our loves in hymeneal bowers!

* . *   *   *

LXIX.

See, thronging the cathedral, sprightly bands
  Of youth and maidens drawn by some sweet spell!
Before the consecrated altar, stands
  ANSELMO, and the charming ISABEL:
The holy Priest hath joined their plighted hands;
  Throughout the dome the marriage anthems swell!
Thus Heaven vests the rights of nuptial life,
And crowns the faithful BRIDE a loving WIFE.

www.ingramcontent.com/pod-product-compliance
Lightning Source LLC
Chambersburg PA
CBHW030343170426
43202CB00010B/1220